www.TheSecureBook.com

Published by Life$^n$ Books, LLC
Copyright © 2012 Rick Dunham
Published 2012
ISBN: 978-1-937033-14-9

Third Printing

For more information:

Life$^n$ Books, LLC
James Van Eerden, Chief Editor
420 Hilton, Suite 100
Stokesdale, North Carolina 27357

# secure.

**Discovering True Financial Freedom**

# RICK DUNHAM

## FOREWORD BY RON BLUE
## INTRODUCTION BY RICH STEARNS

*"This may be the most important book you read this year. It's important because it speaks clearly and concisely to what may be the single most important issue facing the Church in our time: money – how we view it, how we spend it and the influence it has over every aspect of our lives. Rick Dunham has answers for you. His small book is a phenomenal summary of all that Scripture has to say about money and security. Invest just a few hours in reading* Secure *and I promise you that you will never again think about money in the same way. In fact, I plan to read it once a year."*

> **— Rich Stearns, President, World Vision US and author of *The Hole in Our Gospel***

*"The Bible has a lot to say about finances (and Rick Dunham will deftly illuminate all of those passages for you in the pages that follow), but why is it such a sticky subject for believers? I agree with Rick's assertion that it revolves around our desire for security. All of us long for security. And on the surface, that is what money promises.* **The message of Secure is that God cares about every detail of our lives, and every material blessing comes from His hand."**

> **—Jim Daly, President, Focus on the Family and author of *Stronger***

*"Rick, my friend and partner in ministry, sheds light on the spiritual dynamics behind our use and abuse of money in a way – candidly – unlike anything I've ever seen (and I've read a lot about stewardship).* **Intensely biblical, practical and accessible, you will be enriched in reading it, and appreciated in sharing it."**

> **— Pete Briscoe, Senior Pastor, Bent Tree Bible Fellowship, Carrollton, Texas, and President of Telling the Truth Media Ministries**

"Christians must diligently guard their hearts and be clear about the difference between God's economy and the world's economy. In Rick Dunham's book, Secure, he masterfully details God's perspective on finances, stewardship, and where our security needs to rest. With elegant simplicity and his personal testimony, he makes the way to financial peace clear. **This is one handbook for the heart that every believer must keep close and reference often.**"

— Tami Heim, President and CEO of Christian Leadership Alliance

"**Rick Dunham has written** Secure **to help us find our spiritual balance again**. To assist all who want to rise out of the pit of recent meltdowns and find the way of true financial freedom."

— Dr. Jack Graham, Pastor, Prestonwood Baptist Church, Plano, Texas, and Teacher on PowerPoint Ministries with Jack Graham

"Materialism is a disease of the heart and can only be cured by our Lord Jesus Christ. This book, written by my good friend Rick Dunham, goes right to the heart of that issue. **I encourage you to engage with it seriously and very prayerfully.**"

— Ron Blue, President, Kingdom Advisors and author of *Master Your Money*

"My good friend Rick Dunham has written a very powerful yet succinct work on the meaning of, and method to, experiencing victory. **Secure will enable every reader to realize the financial freedom that God intended for each of us to have.**"

— Dr. Tony Evans, Senior Pastor, Oak Cliff Bible Church, Dallas, Texas, and President of The Urban Alternative with Dr. Tony Evans

*"I have told you these things,*
*so that in me you may have peace.*
*In this world you will have trouble.*
*But take heart!*
***I have overcome the world."***
John 16:33

To Judi…

I can't imagine the journey without *you*…
Your wise counsel, your unshakable faith,
your constant encouragement and
your faithful prayers.

# Table of Contents

# Publisher's Preface

*PEACE* CAN SOMETIMES SEEM elusive. *Security,* a kindred quality of the soul, can seem to appear and disappear like a desert mirage.

Some of us are more, or less, risk-averse. But no matter how much risk we are inclined to tolerate, human nature compels all of us to seek security. Even "dare-devils" are seeking security – trying to secure their identity based on a willingness to take a dare.

We can seek security in many places. Fame and fortune and all sorts of fantasies glitter with promise. They leave people wanting, but never content. Even good things that seem God-honoring and enduring will fail us: a spouse, family, friends, church fellowship and the like are gifts that bring deep joy and love to us, but they are not meant to be grasped for the "life balance" that only true security can offer.

Getting the quest for security right is fundamental to a well-lived life. Indeed, our understanding of how we become *secure* tends to shape the way we make decisions, steward wealth, set priorities, and live our lives.

Like you, perhaps, I have journeyed alongside people who have held fast to the anchors of security that this world has to offer. I have watched those anchors give way, and seen the torment caused by putting confidence in something that is not meant to be grasped for security's sake. It is a kind of treachery that causes a deep unsettling of the soul.

Classic autobiographies are classic for two reasons, mainly. The first is that they deal with themes that many people can relate to in their own lives, across different cultures and different times. The second reason is that the author creates for his readers a picture of another soul that is authentic, engaging, and compelling.

This concise book by Rick Dunham offers both. The author's journey through his fair share of life's storms is the backdrop against which he paints a clear image of what it is to be *Secure*, in the only true sense. It is not a rosy lens he gives us, but a clear one. And that is precisely what I needed when I read it for the first time, and perhaps what you need as you read these words right now.

Some years ago, we published a version of the novel called *The Ultimate Gift*. That book has sold millions of copies and been made into an award-winning film by 20th Century Fox. The story contrasts true wealth with the counterfeit versions. Through a powerful but simple narrative, its author Jim Stovall moves readers to consider what it is that makes an inheritance a good and lasting one – or the opposite. It is about the journey into an abundant life.

This book takes you on a journey as well, from Page One. We think it will leave you different and better, and … all in all, quite clear about how you can be *Secure*.

*Jim Van Eerden*
Life $^n$ Books, LLC
*Magnalia Forest, North Carolina*

SECURE

# Foreword
*by Ron Blue*

I HAVE HAD THE PRIVILEGE for more than 30 years to answer thousands of questions about finance and to offer counsel to some of the most generous men and women in God's kingdom. I have also written several books dealing with God's principles of money and money management. I say all of that to simply help you understand my perspective.

In one form or another, the question I get most often is, "How much is enough?" The question behind this question is, "Will I ever be secure financially?"

My answer to the question is best illustrated by an experience I had while traveling in East Africa many years ago. I met a pastor who lived in a one-room mud hut on one acre of ground. He had five children and in meeting one of his children I was sure I had never seen such a peaceful, contented young child. I thought to myself, "Doesn't this child know what she is missing? No Barbie dolls, no Saturday morning cartoons, no Chuck E. Cheese's pizza…."

Later, I asked the pastor what the greatest barrier was to the spread of the gospel in that part of the world. I was expecting him to say money, transportation, communication, or even tribalism. His response was that the greatest barrier to the gospel in his part of the world was materialism. *Materialism?*

He went on to explain that if a man had a mud hut, he wanted a stone hut. If he had a thatch roof, he wanted a metal roof. If he had one acre, he wanted two acres. There was never enough. Immediately, I understood.

Materialism is a disease of the heart and can only be cured by our Lord Jesus Christ.

This book, written by my good friend Rick Dunham, goes right to the heart of that issue. There is a war going on and the god of materialism is struggling against the God of creation. He just doesn't understand that the God of creation has already won the battle.

The only way to experience true security is to have that eternal relationship with God through the Lord Jesus Christ. *It has nothing at all to do with money.* You can never

ever accumulate enough money to be ultimately financially secure. There is far too much uncertainty in a world that is dominated by sin.

In my experience, the only people who are truly free financially understand that God owns it all. The evidence of that belief is in their generosity. It doesn't make any difference whether we live in turbulent times or peaceful times; the only security to be found is in our relationship to God.

My hope and prayer is that untold thousands will take hold of the key to security as outlined by Rick in this book. It is a privilege to write the foreword to *Secure* and I encourage you to engage with it seriously and very prayerfully.

*Ron Blue*

CEO

*Kingdom Advisors*

SECURE

# Introduction
*by Rich Stearns*

THIS MAY BE THE MOST important book you read this year.

It's important because it speaks clearly and concisely to what may be the single most important issue facing the Church in our time: money – how we view it, how we spend it and the influence it has over every aspect of our lives. Money can empower ministries, save lives, and provide God's blessings in a million ways. But money can also corrupt, destroy, cause harm, and damage the human soul.

Follow the money. Anyone who watches TV police dramas or reads crime novels knows that you can uncover secret motives and explain a lot of human behavior if you just 'follow the money.' Jesus understood this well when

He stated *"where your treasure is, there your heart will be also."* In fact, fifteen percent of Jesus' recorded words dealt with money, more than He said about heaven and hell combined. The Bible has more to say about money than faith and prayer combined.

Indeed, if you look at the 'power lines' that flow through our world, money is the 'current' that flows through them. And to carry the metaphor further, we know that power lines are dangerous because the power that runs through them is deadly if precautions are not taken.

Many of Jesus' words about money involved warnings. Jesus recognized that the chief competitor to our dependence on Him is our money. When we have enough cash, food, and possessions, we can become self-reliant. Therefore, money is not seen by God as a benign and neutral thing. Money is power, and power competes with God for supremacy in our lives. Jesus recognized this very thing in the Sermon on the Mount. *"No one can serve two masters. Either you will hate the one and love the other, or you will be devoted to the one and despise the other. You cannot serve both God and money"* (Matthew 6:24).

Note that both God and money are portrayed in a master-slave relationship to the person. Jesus recognized that we will be a slave to one or the other but not to both. In fact, Jesus often talked about money as if it were battery acid – something to handle with extreme caution!

So if money is dangerous to Christians, then Christians in the wealthiest nations live in the most dangerous places of all. In America, we live in a culture dominated by materialism. One definition of materialism is *'an excessive regard for worldly concerns.'* Isn't the American Dream all about worldly concerns and achieving prosperity and success?

Our desire to be wealthy is so great that lottery ticket sales in the U.S. total about $52 billion each year – almost twice as much as our U.S. foreign assistance budget to help poor nations. The apostle Paul issued this stern warning to those who pursue wealth: *"Those who want to get rich fall into temptation and a trap and into many foolish and harmful desires that plunge men into ruin and destruction. For the love of money is a root of all kinds of evil. Some people, eager for money, have wandered from the faith and pierced themselves with many griefs"* (1 Timothy 6:9-10).

But there is another dimension to money that is critical for Christians to understand – it is the fuel that powers every Christian ministry on earth. The Scripture tells us that we are all engaged in a 'clash of kingdoms' in which the evil one is at war with the kingdom of God. We struggle, Paul said, *"not against flesh and blood, but against the rulers, against the authorities, against the powers of this dark world and against the spiritual forces of evil in the heavenly realms"* (Ephesians 6:12).

Simply put, we are servants of the King and the King is at war.

Yet, despite the dangers and the strategic importance of money, we rarely talk about it. We often try to avoid talking about it. I believe that the least preached sermon in America is the one that addresses stewardship and our relationship to money. And yet the choices we make about our money have profound implications for our own spiritual health, the work of the Kingdom and even the fate of the hundreds of millions of our brothers and sisters in Christ who live in desperate poverty on the very edge of life.

Today in our world, one billion people are starving. Four in ten have never heard the gospel. There are fifty million orphaned children in Africa alone. Malaria, AIDS, tuberculosis, water borne diseases and a host of diseases most of us have never heard of, take the lives of some 22,000 children every single day. For lack of just one dollar a year – the cost of bringing clean, safe water to one child – we know that a child dies every fifteen seconds.

You see the choices we make about money are moral choices and they sometimes have life and death consequences. And God cares about the choices we make.

The Lord gave to His Church the Great Commission – to 'make disciples of all nations' – and the Great Commandment – to 'love our neighbors as ourselves' –

and both depend on our money and what we choose to do with it. If giving stopped today, just about every church and ministry would be out of business within sixty days. And if giving were to double or triple, the additional money could change the world for Christ in profound ways.

The questions for you to answer are these: Has money become an idol in your life competing with God? Are you handling money according to good biblical principles? Is money your slave or your master? Are you using your money to support the King – or to live like one?

Rick Dunham has answers for you. His small book is a phenomenal summary of all that Scripture has to say about money and security. Invest just a few hours in reading *Secure* and I promise you that you will never again think about money in the same way. In fact, I plan to read it once a year.

*Rich Stearns*
President
*World Vision*

# CHAPTER 1

# A Wake-Up Call?

AS I WALKED TO MY CAR, I really wondered what I would do now.

Ten months ago things had seemed so perfect. We had been offered a job back in Southern California close to family, found a beautiful new home in a great location, and I had started working with a fast-growing ministry that I loved.

But in the last ten months things had gone from great to, well, a disaster.

The timing of our move ended up being as bad as it gets. It just happened to coincide with the complete collapse of the housing market in the Dallas area. So ten months after we had moved, we still had not been able to sell our house

– no matter what we did. That meant we were carrying two house payments: one for our old house in Dallas and one for our new house in Southern California. As you can imagine, the strain on our finances was pretty enormous.

In addition, a few months after moving back to Southern California, our third child was born … with the typical expenses of a newborn being added to the costs of our young family. And all those expenses along with two house payments had drained us of any savings we had.

Now I was on my way home to tell my wife I had just been fired.

I felt like I had taken a blow that knocked the wind out of me. I also felt like a complete and utter failure with no possible way out of the mess I had created.

Everything I had ever thought about success and money had been completely wiped away. I was stripped clean and was once again starting at zero – or worse yet, in minus territory.

I have thought a lot about that time in my life as I have watched many families lose so much since the beginning of the Global Financial Crisis. A crisis that seems to be becoming a chronic economic problem with no end in sight. As the world economy continues to roil, it creates the typical ripples of most economic crises: a stressed and rigid banking system, a weakened housing market, high unemployment, and a very uncertain future.

Millions are feeling the pain as many continue to be unemployed, others just now losing their jobs, families struggling with strained budgets due to increasing costs or the loss of their dream home ... or both.

I have known their pain.

That day for me, having just been fired, put me into a severe financial crisis. There I was with a young family of five, two mortgages, no job, and deep in debt. Bankruptcy seemed like a speeding locomotive heading straight at me.

There were many sleepless nights crying out to and wrestling with God. "Why me, Lord? I acted in good faith. I trusted You! Where are You when I need You? Is this what I get for serving You? *Where are You?* "

I was desperate, filled with an overwhelming sense of failure and with no solution in sight. In those nights alone with God I would eventually find myself confessing, "I do not know what You are up to, but I do not have any choice but to trust You."

Looking back, what I realize now is that God took me into a financial wilderness to teach me lessons that I could not have learned any other way. He was, in fact, rescuing me from a bondage I did not really understand – *from a misplaced security.*

God used my personal financial disaster and those years in the wilderness to begin a process of reframing my thinking about money and success. He met me at the lowest possible point in my life when I was most vulnerable (and extremely teachable) and gently led me on an amazing journey to a destination that I thought I would never find. He led me to a place of real financial freedom and genuine security. I thought that place did not exist – except, perhaps, for those of great wealth.

Today I cannot help but think that He took me through those years not only to take me to that place, but to help others – perhaps you – who find themselves struggling through some sort of financial crisis. Or have this real fear of the future and whether or not you'll be able to make it financially. I am writing this for those who feel as if they are in financial bondage, and long to be free, secure, and at peace.

What I learned is that God cares deeply about our finances. He really does! In fact, Jesus spent a lot of His ministry addressing the seductive power of money, and explaining why the handling of our money is so important to Him. As Rich Stearns wrote in the Introduction, Jesus talks more about money than heaven and hell combined.

This is a central issue directly impacting our relationship with Him.

I also learned that there are traps that can easily ensnare us and put us into bondage. Consumer debt, financially stretching to maintain a certain lifestyle, presuming on the future and minimizing delayed gratification.

And finally, He showed me the true meaning of what many Christians call *stewardship*.

That is why, in the midst of a financial crisis that has so many Christians in its grip, I feel a sense of excitement and hope. When I look back at my own life and the debilitating financial crisis I experienced, I realize that coming out of the dark night of my economic despair, God brought about a hope and new sense of security, peace, and freedom I never could have anticipated. And it is a great place to be!

Maybe the ongoing financial crisis we are in … and the challenges you are facing … are being used by God to help you reframe your thinking and discover the freedom, peace, and security your heart longs for, and that God wants you to have. I am speaking of a freedom, peace, and security that cannot be swept away by any economic storm or personal financial crisis – no matter how severe.

If that is what you long for, then you have picked up a book that could be very helpful. In the following pages I want to take you on the same journey to discover exactly what I did: that the security God offers you as His child is not dependent on the size of your bank account, the strength of your financial portfolio, or the amount of your paycheck. It is a true financial freedom, a genuine security that can never be taken away.

# CHAPTER 2

# The Starting Point

IN THE DAYS AFTER I was fired I did everything humanly possible to try to get out of the mess I had created. Within a month I had a new job, at about 80% of my former salary. My wife and I worked hard to sell both houses. We even tried to swap our California house for another one the builder had in a different location, but nothing was moving that year.

We were stuck and finally decided to declare bankruptcy when family stepped in and helped, keeping us from going over the edge. For that I will always be grateful.

But day after day God seemed silent, which drove me into the Word and prayer like never before. And it was over the next few years that God began to reveal a truth that I just did not expect to be part of the equation. In fact, it was the furthest thing from my mind. But it is the starting point to discovering real security and true financial freedom.

That truth is this: *You and I are caught up in an all-out spiritual war that is raging every moment of every day.* There are forces of darkness and evil which are aggressively and relentlessly waging war against God's kingdom, and that means you and me, whether we acknowledge it or not.

Every moment … even right now … demonic powers are at work to undermine your effectiveness as a follower of Jesus. They want to continually weaken your relationship with God and render you impotent to impact your world for Christ.

What God went on to show me was that one of the most significant battlefronts in this war – and one that is too often overlooked – is money. I will show you how vital a weapon money is to the forces of evil, but first I want you to come to appreciate, as I have, just how real and intense this war actually is.

In his book, *Waking the Dead*, John Eldredge makes a simple but powerful statement: "Things are not what they seem. This is a world at war." He then goes on to explain:

> *The world in which we live is a combat zone, a violent clash of kingdoms, a bitter struggle unto the death....*
> *You were born into a world at war, and you will live*

*all your days in the midst of a great battle, involving all the forces of heaven and hell and played out here on earth .... Until we come to terms with war as the context of our days, we will not understand life* (pp. 13, 17).

I believe most Christians today give a tip of the hat to the notion of spiritual warfare. They believe in the devil and demons. But in fact, they do not embrace the moment-by-moment reality of spiritual conflict and the fact that Satanic forces are on the offensive to do us spiritual harm. As a result, it does not inform how you and I live as it should.

As C.S. Lewis wrote in *Mere Christianity*:

*One of the things that surprised me when I first read the New Testament seriously was that it talked so much about a Dark Power in the universe—a mighty evil spirit who was held to be the Power behind death and disease and sin.... This universe is at war* (p. 50).

Yes. This universe is at war – a war with eternal consequences. And over and over again the biblical record allows us a glimpse of this war by pulling back the curtain on our physical world. Scripture is replete with examples that, frankly, have become too familiar and end up being just familiar "Bible stories."

## The Beginning of the War

War against Satan was declared by God at the beginning of human history, when in the Garden of Eden He said to the devil:

*"And I will put enmity between you and the woman, and between your offspring and hers; he will crush your head, and you will strike his heel"* (Genesis 3:15).

This war against Satan and his forces of evil was the focal point of Jesus' ministry. In fact, the Bible tells us that defeating Satan was the very purpose Jesus came to earth. John makes this very clear in 1 John 3:8 when He states:

*The reason the Son of God appeared was to destroy the devil's work.*

The life of Jesus was defined by the epic war being waged by the forces of darkness against God and His plan to redeem mankind. And it culminated in His seeming defeat on the cross . . . and His stunning victory when He rose from the dead.

We see this battle play out in the life of Christ in so many ways. But perhaps the greatest evidence of this war was the temptation of Christ.

When we read the account of how Christ was tempted by Satan in the wilderness, we tend to minimize the event by thinking that it was some sort of debate between Jesus and the devil. No. It was a hand-to-hand spiritual struggle. The stakes were the future of all mankind, and the fulfillment of God's kingdom program hung in the balance.

Have you ever noticed that after Satan tempted Jesus by asking Him to turn a stone into bread – in order to make Jesus break His 40-day fast – he then took Jesus to the highest point of the temple, and to a high mountain?

Do you think it was not a fight? Satan came to Jesus at a point of physical weakness to see if he could get Him off His mission. And while Jesus was certainly all-powerful God, He was fully human as well. So it was a battle. If it was not, why did the angels need to come and attend to Jesus after Satan finally left Him?

No, the temptation of Christ was not a simple debate. It was a demonstration to you and me of just how intense the battle was in that moment between the forces of good and evil, between darkness and light. Satan seized a moment to try to thwart the advancement of God's kingdom. It was an all-out effort, which he has undertaken since the moment he rebelled.

Jesus warned us we would be joining in this battle when He assured Peter in Matthew 16:18 about the outcome. He said, *"And I tell you that you are Peter, and on this rock I will build my church, and the gates of Hades will not overcome it."*

It is pretty telling that the focus of Jesus when talking about the building of His Church was that the *"gates of Hades will not overcome it."* Of all the things Jesus could have said, the one thing He had on His mind was the reality of how the forces of hell would come against the Church. They would intensely resist the coming of God's kingdom on this earth. At times, it might even seem as if those forces were indeed overcoming it. But Jesus assures us that Satan's forces will go down in defeat!

Throughout His earthly ministry, Jesus lived with this spiritual war in the forefront of His mind. Over and over we read of Him confronting Satan, driving out demonic powers, and rebuking those under the power of the Evil One – like the religious authorities of His day. And today the forces of hell are arrayed against God's kingdom and they will do everything they can to stop its advancement. *That is our reality.*

We find the thread of this ongoing spiritual battle woven throughout the record of Scripture. Take, for example, the scene as described in Daniel, chapter 10. It is an incredibly fascinating passage that gives us a glimpse into the battle that is constantly raging in the spiritual realm.

Here is what an angel tells Daniel in response to his prayer:

*"Since the first day that you set your mind to gain*

*understanding and to humble yourself before your God, your words were heard, and I have come in response to them. But the prince of the Persian kingdom resisted me twenty-one days. Then Michael, one of the chief princes, came to help me, because I was detained there with the king of Persia"* (Daniel 10:12-13).

The forces of evil, embodied in the prince of the Persian kingdom, stood against the angel sent from God. Those forces fought ferociously to keep the angel away from Daniel for 21 days. In fact, it took the help of Michael, the archangel, for the angel sent by God to finally be victorious over the demonic prince of the Persian kingdom.

Then there is the amazing passage found in 2 Kings 6. In this passage, Elisha the prophet was being pursued by the king of Aram because he was fed up with Elisha. Every time the king set an ambush for the king of Israel, God revealed it to Elisha and Elisha was able to warn the king of Israel to avoid the ambush.

So the king of Aram sent a strong force to capture Elisha. During the night, this strong force surrounded the city, and in the morning Elisha's servant got up early, stepped outside, and that is where we pick up the rest of the story:

*When the servant of the man of God got up and went out early the next morning, an army with horses and*

*chariots had surrounded the city. "Oh, my lord, what
shall we do?" the servant asked. "Don't be afraid,"
the prophet answered. "Those who are with us are
more than those who are with them." And Elisha
prayed, "O LORD, open his eyes so he may see." Then
the LORD opened the servant's eyes, and he looked
and saw the hills full of horses and chariots of fire all
around Elisha* (2 Kings 6:15-17).

Can you imagine what Elisha's servant must have
felt when he stepped outside that morning to get a fresh
breath of air? When he opened the door and saw the strong
force that the king of Aram had sent, I am sure the blood
drained from his head, his knees got weak, and he probably
whispered a few expletives under his breath.

But Elisha coolly reassures his servant, "Our forces
outnumber those guys." And you have to believe that
Elisha's servant was most likely thinking, "This old prophet
has finally lost his marbles. He is raving mad. I know he
was never good at the math thing, but really, I am counting
two of us and hundreds of them! The last time I checked,
*hundreds outnumber . . . two.*"

That is when the Lord revealed the host of angelic
beings armed and ready to go to battle at Elisha's request,
with the hills "full of horses and chariots of fire all around
Elisha." Angelic forces were arrayed and ready to take on

the forces that would stand in the way of God's kingdom purposes. That was their mission.

Elisha and his servant saw the reality of the spiritual war as the forces of evil sought to thwart God's kingdom advancement.

In our day-to-day experiences, it is so hard for us to live with a conscious understanding of the spiritual battle that impacts every part of our lives. There are spiritual forces of evil at work doing all they can to stop God's purposes and to hamper His kingdom initiatives. Nonetheless, God is actively engaging those forces to bring about the ultimate redemption of His creation. And He will be victorious. *His is the winning side.*

The culmination of this war is unveiled in the last book of the Bible, Revelation. This prophetic vision outlines God's plan for the end of human history and the ultimate destruction of the forces of evil when Jesus will forever crush Satan and his kingdom of darkness. In Revelation, chapter 12 (vv. 7-8, 17), we are given insight into the reality of the spiritual battle and how Satan's energy is focused on making war against you and me:

> *And there was war in heaven. Michael and his angels fought against the dragon, and the dragon and his angels fought back. But he was not strong enough, and they lost their place in heaven. Then the dragon*

*was enraged at the woman and went off to make war against the rest of her offspring—those who obey God's commandments and hold to the testimony of Jesus.*

Satan, the dragon, is an avowed enemy of Jesus and is consumed with rage against the Church of Jesus Christ and is obsessed with making war against you and me. He has done … is doing … and will do anything in his power to destroy God's purposes and stop the advancement of His kingdom. It is this all-out war in the spiritual realm that is the reality and the framework for our lives today, whether we acknowledge it or not.

## A People Under Orders

Because we are at war with the forces of evil, God has made us a people under orders. Perhaps the simplest expression of those orders is found in Acts 26, in which Jesus gives Paul this mandate:

*"'… I am sending you to them to open their eyes and turn them from darkness to light, and from the power of Satan to God, so that they may receive forgiveness of sins and a place among those who are sanctified by faith in me'"* (vv. 17-18).

Jesus made clear to Paul that his orders from that day forward were to engage the forces of darkness: to move people from the power and dominion of Satan to the power and dominion of God.

*And that is our purpose today.*

God has called you and me to a rescue mission. We are a people "under orders" as part of His forces to liberate men, women, and children from the power of Satan and his kingdom of darkness and death, bringing them into God's kingdom of light. As Paul recounts in Ephesians 2:

*As for you, you were dead in your transgressions and sins, in which you used to live when you followed the ways of this world and of the ruler of the kingdom of the air, the spirit who is now at work in those who are disobedient* (vv. 1-2).

But do not think for a moment that Satan will not put up a fight! That is why Peter warns us in 1 Peter 5:

*Be self-controlled and alert. Your enemy the devil prowls around like a roaring lion looking for someone to devour* (v. 8).

And it is also why Paul reminds us in Ephesians 6:10-12 that the true field of battle is in the spiritual realm:

*Finally, be strong in the Lord and in His mighty power. Put on the full armor of God so that you can take your stand against the devil's schemes. For our struggle is not against flesh and blood, but against the rulers, against the authorities, against the powers of*

*this dark world and against the spiritual forces of evil*
*in the heavenly realms.*

We are in a cosmic war. We must understand that this epic spiritual struggle is the reality that is playing out in our world today. And Satan, being the master deceiver, will do all he can to put *you* on the sidelines and render *you* impotent in this battle.

And that is where money comes into play, because it is one of the Enemy's most powerful weapons. Satan wants you and me to replace God as our source of security with the false security of money. When he seduces us to think this way, he keeps us from advancing God's kingdom as we should. But, more importantly, *he keeps us from fully following after God.*

As Jesus warned, wherever our treasure is, that is where our heart will be. If our priority is in the stuff of the here-and-now, then that is where our heart will be. It will not be on kingdom matters – which means Satan has succeeded in undermining our impact as followers of Christ.

*You just cannot worship God AND money. It is one or the other.*

That is why the whole issue of money and giving is such a crucial battlefront in the spiritual struggle of our day. And that is why it is vital that we have a true biblical understanding of money since it represents such a key battlefront in the cosmic war in which we are presently engaged.

**CHAPTER 3**

# Our Misplaced Security

I WILL NEVER FORGET that night.

It was 20 years after we had gone through the disaster of the loss of my job. It had been a real struggle, but God had finally brought us out of that wilderness and by His grace, we had fully recovered. In fact, we had experienced financial success we never could have expected or imagined.

But now my wife and I sat over dinner at our favorite Italian restaurant with the situation feeling eerily the same. We were both a bit stunned as I had just come from the attorney's office where I had been in long, arduous meetings trying to negotiate the appropriate end to a business relationship.

Before I left the attorney's office he looked at me and said, "Rick, you and Judi need to be prepared to lose everything." And now I was breaking the news to my wife.

"Sheesh, here we go again!" I thought.

That night at dinner is indelibly etched into my memory. As the words fell from my mouth, we just looked at each other. Then something happened that neither Judi nor I ever expected or have since been able to explain. An enormous and unspeakable peace came over both of us.

In that moment, we realized how unimportant money really is to our security, our sense of peace, and even to our happiness. As we talked, we sensed a freedom that was entirely unexpected.

While I had thought that the financial struggle 20 years previous was a struggle due to the lack of money, debt, and too many expenses, the real struggle was my misplaced trust in money to bring me true peace and security. It only took me 20 years of wandering – and the potential for it all to be stripped away – for me to finally figure it out.

I have to say that I was shocked. I really was. I just did not expect to experience such peace at a time when everything seemed so desperately uncertain. I did not anticipate that I would (or could) sense such security when things were so *insecure*. But in that moment, God gently brought me to the realization that God alone is the only truly secure thing I have in life, and that money can never offer that kind of security. I think Judi was already there… but that night did it for me.

No matter how bad it might get, I could trust God. *Fully.* You simply cannot say the same thing about money, and the other things to which we tend to cling. In fact, up until that evening, I thought money could provide some source of security. It just stands to reason, does it not? But in the midst of that conversation, I realized just how unstable and fleeting money really is.

As I thought about it later, I realized that money is an amazingly powerful force in our lives – indeed, much greater than we are often willing to admit. From rich to poor, no one is immune from its all-consuming reach.

It wields its power and control over the poor who struggle just to put food on the table. It provides a false hope to those reaching for the golden ring of prosperity. And it deceives the rich into believing they have freedom – when, in fact, the more money they have, the easier it is to fall under the spell of its power and influence!

It is an amazing irony, but money is the one thing that can give us freedom and put us in bondage all at the same time.

Money can be a cruel master that can impact every part of life. Yet most people willingly serve this unforgiving god, believing the promises it always fails to deliver. No wonder the Bible talks so much about money. No wonder Jesus took time to deal directly with the seductive nature of its power and influence.

And no wonder it is such a major weapon of Satan in his war against God's kingdom.

For the most part, the biblical teaching regarding money has failed to seep into the fabric of Christianity in the West. If we are brutally honest, our view of money as followers of Christ has been formed by our capitalistic and consumer-focused societies and is not all that different than that of our secular culture. And we demonstrate that every day in how we handle our money.

The sad result is that we have a view of money that is more culturally informed than it is biblically informed, and we place our faith in it to provide us security, rather than placing faith in God for our security. This is much to Satan's delight and our Heavenly Father's distress.

One reason our view of money as Christians is not biblically informed is that indirectly (or sometimes directly) we make sure the pastor knows that to talk about money is "off limits." We are willing to be taught how to live in the power of the Holy Spirit, how to make our marriages stronger, how to parent better, how to be godly leaders, how to stand for truth and justice in our world, and how to be socially-minded.

But we are not real happy when money is the focus of teaching from the pulpit. That is especially true when it comes to giving. That is over the line. That is personal. That is "none of your business."

The consequence is that most Christians relegate their view of giving to tithing. As a result, we fail to understand the fundamental role money plays in becoming a wholly devoted follower of Jesus Christ. We do not realize that how we handle money, including giving, is in fact a critical part of what takes us to that deeper walk with God that you and I both long to experience.

Instead, the exercise of giving for most of us is more like tipping God than anything else. If you think that is a bit of an overstatement, consider this:

> *According to Center on Philanthropy statistics for 2008, only 64.4% of Baptists gave anything during that year. And of those who gave, the average amount of giving to religion was only 2% of their income.*[1]

That is a tip. *And a bad one, at that.*

What is especially sad is that this minimal giving is prominent across *all* denominations. No membership of any

---

[1] 2008 study conducted by Patrick Rooney, Interim Director of The Center on Philanthropy, Indiana University.

Christian denomination comes close to giving 10% of their income to religious organizations or churches. In fact, as of this writing, less than 8% of households in America give 10% or more to religion.[2] Wow.

What I came to realize in my journey was that I just did not have a true biblical view of money and giving. Harsh as it may seem, the issue of giving and how we handle money is not viewed by most of us as a non-negotiable part of our personal relationship with Christ. It is trumped by things like Bible reading, prayer, accountability to others, worship, mission trips, and attending small group studies – the endless list of things we focus on to grow spiritually and become "whole-hearted followers" of Jesus.

While all of these exercises are important as you and I seek to grow in our spiritual walk, I now believe we cannot become wholly devoted followers of Jesus Christ, we cannot mature as Christians, we cannot enjoy a truly intimate relationship with God . . . if we fail to view and therefore handle money as God has outlined in His Word.

It is simple, yet profound. Our money and our hearts are tethered together with an unbreakable cord. As I mentioned earlier, Jesus said it simply and powerfully:

*". . . where your treasure is, there your heart will be also."*

Our treasure and our hearts are inextricably tied together. There are no exceptions. None. And if we want to

---

[2] COPPS 2005

fully follow after Jesus Christ, then we cannot take how we handle our money out of the discipleship equation.

Satan knows this – which is why, I am convinced, he has used money so successfully as a potent weapon in his war against God and his people. I think too many of us as followers of Christ have been deceived into believing that money is not really a central part of our walk with God. And for too many, it has become a greater source of security than God Himself.

I think this is one reason why Jesus went on to say:

*"No one can serve two masters. Either he will hate the one and love the other, or he will be devoted to the one and despise the other. You cannot serve both God and Money"* (Matthew 6:24).

It is fascinating that the word *money* has its origins in the Roman goddess Juno. A title for her was Moneta ("she who warns"), and this title was attributed to coins that were minted in or near her temple.[3]

It is fitting that the term *money* is related to a Roman goddess. Any honest observer of our Western world will recognize that we serve and worship money. We live in societies that are based on a worldview that is driven by money and consumerism, and therefore informs how people

---

[3] Sourced through Wikipedia

in those societies handle their money . . . including the vast majority of Christians.

This is not to say that I am an anti-capitalist. I am not. It has been the engine that has best driven economies and built great nations. But Adam Smith, who was a theologian first and an economist second, was more than insightful when he contended that *The Wealth of Nations* must be complemented by the spiritual formation of people. Capitalism creates a stunning forest of trees, but without spiritual formation it is a forest of trees without roots. This is why Smith considered his book, *A Theory of Moral Sentiments*, as a necessary companion to his more famous treatise.

The capitalistic spirit often leads to consumerism, and unbridled consumerism is based on a humanistic view of God's world. This kind of consumerism comes from and creates a worldview that is anchored in the here-and-now. It most often encourages people to accumulate capital for self-serving and self-glorifying purposes, like so many mansions in America's suburbia that are shrines to Mammon. This is the context for our modern day Baal – the god that the masses worship. People believe that this god will bring security and good fortune.

But they are wrong. Sincerely wrong.

When I lost my job, I thought our problem was that we were financially over-extended and in debt, and that money could fix the mess that we were in. I believed that if we could just get our hands on more money, we would be secure. And 20 years later, when we didn't have a financial concern and we thought we *were* secure, we found ourselves in the same exact place. Money – whether you have a lot of it or a little of it – can be ripped away from you in but a moment.

Money can never be a source of genuine security; only God can be that.

On that evening long ago, my wife and I discovered this liberating truth. And I think God wants to use the meltdown of our world economy and the resulting financial struggles of nations, markets, economies, and households to help others – perhaps you – learn this same truth.

Money promises a security it can never deliver. Never.

Our hearts have been seduced and ensnared by the promise of freedom, peace, and security when, in fact, money only turns our hearts away from fully following after God and His purposes.

That is why I believe the financial earthquake and the extended recession after it, like every economic upheaval, is a clear and vibrant wake-up call to the Church. It challenges our view of money and consumerism. It questions where we have placed our faith and trust. And it calls you and me to honestly evaluate to what degree we have succumbed to the hypnotizing seduction of money.

The lethal danger is that money provides a false sense of security that will keep us from a whole-hearted devotion to God. Jesus constantly warned against this trap. In Luke 12:15-21, He exposed the greed that is a natural inclination of our hearts as we pursue the security that we believe money will provide.

> *Then he said to them, "Watch out! Be on your guard against all kinds of greed; a man's life does not consist in the abundance of his possessions." And he told them this parable: "The ground of a certain rich man produced a good crop. He thought to himself, 'What shall I do? I have no place to store my crops.' Then he said, 'This is what I'll do. I will tear down my barns and build bigger ones, and there I will store all my grain and my goods. And I'll say to myself, "You have plenty of good things laid up for many years. Take life easy; eat, drink and be merry."' But God said to him, 'You fool! This very night your life will be demanded from you. Then who will get what you have prepared for yourself?' This is how it will be with anyone who stores up things for himself but is not rich toward God."*

The sad reality of this parable is that it has played itself out in too many lives. And I dare say that there are countless Christians today who are in danger of making the same mistake. Why? Because this is the natural bent of our hearts. We really do believe that money is a source of security greater than God Himself. It *feels* a whole lot more secure and a lot wiser to build a bigger portfolio, and it *feels* a lot safer to give priority to the stuff of the here-and-now.

This issue of security was the problem that also confronted the rich ruler in Luke 18:18-23. Before we read that passage, though, it is helpful to pause and think about the description Luke gives to this man.

It's clear that this guy was loaded, a leader in the community, and morally upright. Other passages tell us he was young and was eagerly seeking Christ's insights into what it took to gain eternal life. Even with his position of power, his immense wealth, and his moral uprightness, he had this nagging question of what it took to make certain that he had eternal life. That's when we pick up the story…

*A certain ruler asked him, "Good teacher, what must I do to inherit eternal life?" "Why do you call me good?" Jesus answered. "No one is good – except God alone. You know the commandments: 'Do not commit adultery, do not murder, do not steal, do not give false testimony, honor your father and mother.'" "All these*

*I have kept since I was a boy," he said. When Jesus heard this, he said to him, "You still lack one thing. Sell everything you have and give to the poor, and you will have treasure in heaven. Then come, follow me." When he heard this, he became very sad, because he was a man of great wealth.*

Did you notice what was missing in the commandments that Jesus gave the young ruler to follow? The first and most important, *"You shall have no other gods before me."* Jesus deliberately omitted the most important of all commandments, to love God above all else. That seems a bit odd because on another occasion, when asked about the most important commandment, Jesus was quick to say: *"Love the Lord your God with all your heart and with all your soul and with all your mind.' This is the first and greatest commandment"* (Matthew 22:37-38).

So why did Jesus omit this command and focus on the others? Because He knew that this young, wealthy leader had indeed kept the commandments he listed but failed on the first and most important. Jesus knew the real issue for the rich young ruler was a matter of the heart. Money was his god. It was the source of his security. And he had placed it before his devotion to God.

So instead of quoting the first commandment, Jesus simply went to the heart of that commandment and told him to go sell everything he had and give it to the poor and follow Him. Then he would have treasure in heaven. Jesus was simply saying, "Stop trusting in your stuff and start trusting in me!"

Now, Jesus' point is not that money is bad and we should all go sell everything we have and live the life of a pauper. I believe this story is here to show us that money will naturally become our source of security – our god – indeed, the idol which replaces God. Riches are that strong and seductive.

Money is so alluring that Moses warned the nation of Israel when they were about to go into the Promised Land about it. *"Do not covet the silver and gold on them* [the idols], *and do not take it for yourselves, or you will be ensnared by it"* (Deuteronomy 7:25).

Likewise, for this same reason, Paul directs Timothy to *"command those who are rich in this present world to not be arrogant nor to put their hope in wealth, which is so uncertain, but to put their hope in God, who richly provides us with everything for our enjoyment"* (1 Timothy 6:17).

God knows that money has the power to turn our hearts away from Him and His kingdom purposes because our hearts are inclined to put our "hope" in money. And our hearts will always follow where we put our treasure. So if our priority is to build a bigger and better portfolio, or accumulate possessions – giving the here-and-now priority over the eternal – then our hearts cannot fully follow God.

That is the truth straight from our Savior's lips.

Yet, as it has been for me, I suspect this may be a struggle for you. This is a very real danger for us as Christians, even as serious followers of Christ. It is so easy to fall for the seduction of the Evil One and allow our hearts to be given to money above God: to allow our lives to be driven more by consumerism than by genuine, biblical stewardship (a concept we will talk about later in this book).

I can just imagine the echo of Satan's laughter across the spiritual realm as he successfully seduces Christian after Christian into believing the lie of money's promise of security, freedom, and happiness, moving their hearts away from fully following after God. My question to you today is this: *Has he succeeded in your life?*

# CHAPTER 4

# The Biblical View of Money

AS SATAN SEEKS TO SEDUCE you and me into following after the god of money, he will work hard to keep us from aligning our view of money with God's. So it is crucial for you and me to understand how God views money.

Solomon's wise words in Ecclesiastes 5 are a good beginning point.

As you probably know, Ecclesiastes is Solomon's record of how he tested and probed the facets of life to see what would bring him lasting satisfaction. One of these life facets probed by Solomon, then the world's richest man, was wealth. It is remarkable to ponder the conclusions of his intensive consideration of money, and the stuff it buys.

First, Solomon affirms that God is the One who blesses a person with wealth. In Ecclesiastes 5:19, he says:

*Moreover, when God gives any man wealth and possessions, and enables him to enjoy them, to accept his lot and be happy in his work – this is a gift of God.*

God is the giver of wealth. This makes sense. If God owns it all, then it stands to reason that our wealth is just part of what God already owns. This truth is a driving principle for David, as recorded in 1 Chronicles 29:11-14:

*"Yours, O LORD, is the greatness and the power and the glory and the majesty and the splendor, for everything in heaven and earth is yours. Yours, O LORD, is the kingdom; you are exalted as head over all.*

*"Wealth and honor come from you; you are the ruler of all things. In your hands are strength and power to exalt and give strength to all.*

*"Now, our God, we give you thanks, and praise your glorious name.*

*"But who am I, and who are my people, that we should be able to give as generously as this? Everything comes from you, and we have given you only what comes from your hand."*

God owns it all and any wealth that you or I might acquire comes from God's own treasure store.

But Solomon makes another point in Ecclesiastes 5:19. He says that God expects us to enjoy what He has given us. When God gives wealth, He gives the power to enjoy it. So whatever wealth that we might have, we need to see it as a gift from God and not feel guilty about what He has given us.

However, Solomon makes clear that the person whose life is driven by money will never be satisfied because money cannot deliver lasting, ultimate satisfaction. He writes in Ecclesiastes 5:10-11:

> *Whoever loves money never has money enough; whoever loves wealth is never satisfied with his income. This too is meaningless. As goods increase, so do those who consume them. And what benefit are they to the owner except to feast his eyes on them?*

God may give you wealth and the power to enjoy it, but you will never be satisfied if your life is driven by the desire for wealth. This is one of the major seductions of the Evil One. He will subtly move you from understanding that God is giving you the power to enjoy your wealth, to thinking that wealth itself provides that enjoyment. And before you know it, wealth becomes the driving desire of your heart, ultimately keeping God from gaining your whole-hearted devotion.

Thankfully, in these verses Solomon tells us why money cannot bring ultimate satisfaction. First, there's never enough! No matter how wealthy you are, *there is never enough.*

The story goes that somebody once asked John D. Rockefeller how much money is enough. His response? "One dollar more!" We all have experienced that long-awaited raise, only to wonder what happened to it after we had paid the bills. Money always seems to be in short supply when it is the ultimate thing for which we long.

Second, money cannot bring ultimate satisfaction because it is temporal. It is vanity to love money because it will ultimately disappear. If accumulating wealth is your sole or primary life ambition, then you are driven by the temporal – not the eternal. And you will never know true happiness or lasting satisfaction.

Money can never bring eternal joy, happiness, or satisfaction. That joy, happiness, and satisfaction can only come when it is given away, invested in God's eternal purposes.

Solomon understood the seductive power of money to mislead people into a false sense of security. He understood that money makes promises that it always fails to deliver.

The recent Global Financial Crisis, like all downturns in any age, is a great lesson on the reality that money is unstable.

It is not a sound source of security. If you stake the security of your future on your fortune, you will be sorely disappointed and vulnerable.

I am struck by how balanced Solomon is in this chapter of Ecclesiastes. On the one hand, he wants us to understand that whatever God does give, He empowers us to enjoy; and that wealth is not a bad thing. But on the other hand, he wants us to recognize that money is temporal and that we should never be seduced into believing that it can bring us security and satisfaction. It should never be a driving force in our lives.

## Treasuring the Right Treasures

Jesus also deals directly with the futility of a life driven by accumulating wealth, which takes us back to Matthew 6:19-24. Read carefully what He says:

> *"Do not store up for yourselves treasures on earth, where moth and rust destroy, and where thieves break in and steal. But store up for yourselves treasures in heaven, where moth and rust do not destroy, and where thieves do not break in and steal. For where your treasure is, there your heart will be also.*

> *"The eye is the lamp of the body. If your eyes are good, your whole body will be full of light. But if your eyes*

*are bad, your whole body will be full of darkness. If then the light within you is darkness, how great is that darkness!*

*"No one can serve two masters. Either he will hate the one and love the other, or he will be devoted to the one and despise the other. You cannot serve both God and Money."*

It is clear that Jesus recognized that the accumulation of wealth is a natural driver of the human heart. This is why Christ uses the word *treasures* rather than the word *money.*

Treasures deal with the issues of the heart. And God knows the degree to which we treasure money is the degree to which it has captured our heart. For when our hearts "treasure up treasure" (that is the literal translation), God cannot have our whole heart.

We *will* accumulate the stuff we treasure. The only question is where. If we hoard our money and accumulate the stuff of earth, it is temporary. If we invest our money in Kingdom efforts and accumulate the stuff of heaven, it is permanent and eternal – with implications that can only be measured on an infinite scale. When that is our focus, God will have our whole heart, which is what He treasures.

Let's look again at verses 22-23 of Matthew chapter 6:

*"The eye is the lamp of the body. If your eyes are good, your whole body will be full of light. But if your eyes*

*are bad, your whole body will be full of darkness. If then the light within you is darkness, how great is that darkness!"*

This seemed, at first, a bit strange to me. And a bit confusing. What point is Jesus trying to make? Here is the truth I think Christ is hammering home: *If you have the wrong focus, you are in big trouble.* If the light – the thing you believe is right and are focused on to guide you and give you direction – is faulty, deceptive, and ineffective, you are in big trouble!

So if your view of money is messed up, if your relationship with wealth and treasure is perverted, and if you believe money will provide you the security your heart longs for, then you are really deceived. It's like following signals flashing in the distance that are designed to deceive you, which only lead you further and further into a deep darkness.

That is why Jesus goes on to say what He does in the next ten verses. In Matthew 6:25-34, Jesus drives home the point that the Father is the only true source of security. Read His words carefully as He forcefully makes the point that God – not money – is the ONLY thing that you can trust to provide for your wellbeing:

*"Therefore I tell you, do not worry about your life, what you will eat or drink; or about your body, what*

*you will wear. Is not life more important than food, and the body more important than clothes? Look at the birds of the air; they do not sow or reap or store away in barns, and yet your heavenly Father feeds them. Are you not much more valuable than they? Who of you by worrying can add a single hour to his life?*

*"And why do you worry about clothes? See how the lilies of the field grow. They do not labor or spin. Yet I tell you that not even Solomon in all his splendor was dressed like one of these. If that is how God clothes the grass of the field, which is here today and tomorrow is thrown into the fire, will he not much more clothe you, O you of little faith? So do not worry, saying, 'What shall we eat?' or 'What shall we drink?' or 'What shall we wear?' For the pagans run after all these things, and your heavenly Father knows that you need them. But seek first his kingdom and his righteousness, and all these things will be given to you as well. Therefore do not worry about tomorrow, for tomorrow will worry about itself. Each day has enough trouble of its own."*

You have to ask why Jesus would have gone to the lengths He did to stress this point after His poignant and very direct admonition that you and I cannot serve God and money, and that our hearts will follow after the place where we put our treasure.

I think the answer is clear. *He knows our hearts.* He understands that we will, in fact, worry about this kind of stuff, and in doing so will end up placing our priority on earthly rather than heavenly objects. We will give money the place only God should occupy in providing for our security, resulting in a reduced investment in the Father's kingdom work and something less than a whole-hearted commitment to Him.

So here is the question: Have you bought the lie? Have you been seduced into believing that money is really your source of security rather than God? That it is more trustworthy than He is? If so, the next passage might help you understand just how important it is for you, as God's child, to embrace His view of money.

## The Accountability of Stewardship

In Matthew 25:14-30, Christ takes great pains to show the importance of embracing His view of money. In this passage, He wants us to understand the accountability we have as stewards of what He has entrusted to us.

> *Again, it will be like a man going on a journey, who called his servants and entrusted his property to them. To one he gave five talents of money, to another two*

*talents, and to another one talent, each according to his ability. Then he went on his journey. The man who had received the five talents went at once and put his money to work and gained five more. So also, the one with the two talents gained two more. But the man who had received the one talent went off, dug a hole in the ground and hid his master's money.*

*After a long time the master of those servants returned and settled accounts with them. The man who had received the five talents brought the other five. "Master," he said, "you entrusted me with five talents. See, I have gained five more."*

*His master replied, "Well done, good and faithful servant! You have been faithful with a few things; I will put you in charge of many things. Come and share your master's happiness!"*

*The man with the two talents also came. "Master," he said, "you entrusted me with two talents; see, I have gained two more."*

*His master replied, "Well done, good and faithful servant! You have been faithful with a few things; I will put you in charge of many things. Come and share your master's happiness!"*

*Then the man who had received the one talent came. "Master," he said, "I knew that you are a hard man, harvesting where you have not sown and gathering where you have not scattered seed. So I was afraid and went out and hid your talent in the ground. See, here is what belongs to you."*

*His master replied, "You wicked, lazy servant! So you knew that I harvest where I have not sown and gather where I have not scattered seed? Well then, you should have put my money on deposit with the bankers, so that when I returned I would have received it back with interest.*

*"Take the talent from him and give it to the one who has the ten talents. For everyone who has will be given more, and he will have an abundance. Whoever does not have, even what he has will be taken from him. And throw that worthless servant outside, into the darkness, where there will be weeping and gnashing of teeth."*

So what is Jesus' point? God views the money He has entrusted to us as a stewardship. And if we are stewards, that means we do not own the wealth we have because a steward – by definition – does not own what he manages. In fact, a steward becomes a bad steward when he puts his own interests ahead of those of his Master.

What that means for us is pretty profound. It means that *all* of what we have is His, not just 10%. And He has entrusted His resources to you and me expecting that we will effectively invest our resources for maximum return for the kingdom.

This is something that God takes very seriously. In fact, Jesus makes the point over and over in this parable that He will ultimately hold us accountable for how well we have invested what He has put into our trust.

This is a crucial passage to understanding God's view of how we handle the resources He has put into our trust. So let's dive more deeply into it.

# CHAPTER 5

# The Myth of Stewardship

THOUGH IT IS PAINFUL to admit, before my wife and I faced the possibility of bankruptcy a *second* time I thought we fully understood stewardship. But as the months and years have gone by since that pivotal night I have come to realize that we really didn't understand stewardship from God's point of view.

Part of that enlightenment has come as a result of understanding that stewardship is, in fact, a strategic battle line which Satan has chosen to use to try and destroy the effectiveness of God's people and undermine their relationship with their Savior. This battle line is nearly always overlooked. It is a place where the forces of evil are enjoying victory after victory over God's children – to the detriment of God's kingdom work and His children.

How we steward God's resources, how we use what God has entrusted to us to create the greatest possible impact for the kingdom, is a major focal point in Satan's battle strategy. Why?

First, because the ultimate outworking of stewardship is the financial support of God's kingdom work, which is central to the fulfillment of God's purposes here on earth. And second, because it directly impacts our relationship with God.

But before we can become effective givers, we need to first understand what stewardship really is. Stewardship of what God has placed into our trust is so much more than just "tithing." It is the basis upon which effective giving to God's kingdom work actually takes place. That is why it is so important to dive more deeply into this idea of stewardship. Especially since the conventional Christian view of stewardship is a myth.

### Biblical Stewardship

Stewardship is one of the well-worn words of Christendom. The word evokes a lot of different thoughts. And it is without question one of the most important issues facing Christians today, because our view of stewardship ultimately informs how we view our resources and, as a result, what we do with those resources – especially in relation to driving forward God's kingdom purposes.

But I think most Christians get the essence of stewardship wrong. They believe in a myth of what stewardship really is.

So what is the myth of stewardship? It is the belief that stewardship is giving God a portion of what we have and that the rest is ours to do with as we please.

I believe most Christians today believe that if you give God a bit of what you have, then you have been a good steward. They equate stewardship with "tithing."

Naturally, this begs the question of how the Bible defines stewardship. I think we need to go back to the parable of the talents in Matthew 25 to discover what biblical stewardship really is.

In this particular parable, Jesus says that the kingdom of heaven is *like* a man who goes on a journey and trusts his possessions into his servants' hands. Christ wants His disciples to understand that He, the Master, is about to go on a journey and He's planning on entrusting them (and ultimately you and me) with kingdom resources. And when He returns, He will hold us accountable for how we handle what He has put into our trust.

As you read this passage, what do you think the Master expects of His stewards? How would you define stewardship?

Here's how I think Jesus is defining stewardship based on this parable:

> *Stewardship is the wise and effective investment of all the resources the Master has entrusted to us in order to produce the best possible return for Him and for His kingdom.*

Take a moment to re-read that definition. You can see that stewardship is not just about giving A BIT of what we have to the church. Tithing is not stewardship. There is an enormous difference between a mindset that considers a tithe or offering as stewardship and a mindset that considers ALL that we have as something we must steward for the Master.

This means stewardship is not content with the goal of becoming more generous either – i.e., of giving a bigger portion of what we have. Why? Because stewardship has a radical, holistic view of the resources God has entrusted to us and lives with a mindset to *maximize* the use of *all* those resources for God's glory. When that happens, generosity becomes a natural outcome of stewardship, not a goal.

The classic catechisms of the historic Christian faith teach us that the chief aim of man "is to glorify God and enjoy Him forever." How we steward what God has put into our trust … our generosity toward God in and through our stewardship … is an essential aspect of this. Anything less diminishes the glory we bring to God.

Stewardship understood in this way is not about expense management – doing everything on the cheap in order to conserve what we have. Stewardship is *investment* management, not expense management. It seeks to most wisely and effectively invest ALL that God has entrusted to us for the greatest possible return for His glory, for the advancement of His kingdom.

I believe this parable teaches us six principles that can help us understand God's view of stewardship. When we apply these principles, they will help us become truly effective stewards of what God has entrusted to us.

## 1. Stewardship understands that the Master will hold us accountable for how we have managed *everything* in our trust.

Biblical stewards are all in. They see *all* that they have as the property of the Master. Notice that the good steward "went at once and put his money to work and gained five more." Not part, but ALL.

Effective stewardship is driven by an understanding that stewardship is not about how a portion of what we have is invested, but how well *everything* is invested for the Master. That means stewardship is not to be equated solely with giving, although that is a central part of stewardship. Rather, stewardship is to be equated with how well we use all that God has given to us to advance His kingdom.

Do you remember the story when Mary anointed the feet of Jesus with incredibly expensive perfume? I think it is a fairly important lesson on stewardship. It is found in John 12:1-7:

> *Six days before the Passover, Jesus arrived at Bethany, where Lazarus lived, whom Jesus had raised from the dead. Here a dinner was given in Jesus' honor. Martha served, while Lazarus was among those reclining at the table with him. Then Mary took about a pint of pure nard, an expensive perfume; she poured it on Jesus' feet and wiped his feet with her hair. And the house was filled with the fragrance of the perfume.*
>
> *But one of his disciples, Judas Iscariot, who was later to betray him, objected, "Why wasn't this perfume sold and the money given to the poor? It was worth a year's wages." He did not say this because he cared about the poor but because he was a thief; as keeper of the money bag, he used to help himself to what was put into it.*
>
> *"Leave her alone," Jesus replied. "It was intended that she should save this perfume for the day of my burial."*

Before we get too judgmental, I think many Christians would have the same reaction as the disciples. Evangelical emails would have been flying about the way Mary had wasted a year's wages!

But Jesus affirms the use of that expensive perfume in this way. He did not see it as a waste, but rather saw it as a great investment because it was being used to fulfill God's kingdom purpose. All of it. Mary was all in.

Nothing is ever wasted – no matter how extravagant it might appear – when it is being invested or used to advance God's glory. It is all His anyway, so the more we invest, the better! And sometimes that looks completely different from our tax-deductible contributions.

When you understand that God owns it all and is looking to you to steward ALL of what He has given to you, it changes the way you look at how you use your money, time, and resources.

- You want to get out of debt – *and stay out of debt.*

- You use some of your money to take your wife away for a romantic weekend to strengthen your marriage because you understand the priority God places on marriage.

- You honestly do not care about how your neighbors or friends feel about the home you live in or the car you drive.

- You work toward a long-term goal of giving as much as you can to the church and to advance God's kingdom work.

- You help the neighbor or family member in need – even though it may reduce your tax-deductible donations for the year.

- You splurge and throw your spouse a party he or she will never forget for his or her 40th birthday.
- You take your family on an annual vacation to build vital relationships with your kids even though it requires you to sacrifice in other areas.

The list could go on. But I think you get the point. Stewardship involves a macro view of how you use your money, not just the micro view of tithing. It is driven by seeing it all as God's. Do you?

**2. Stewardship has a sense of urgency to it.**

Did you notice that the one servant who was given five talents went out *at once* and put those talents to work? Biblical stewardship has a sense of urgency to it: an urgency about how we invest the resources that God has put into our trust. It is not lazy, undisciplined, or apathetic in how money is used.

The implication, obviously, is that a good steward is pushing things forward by proactively investing what God has given to him or her with the goal of seeing the best possible return for the kingdom.

The Macedonian church mentioned in 2 Corinthians 8 is a great example of this attitude and posture. In this passage Paul tells the Corinthians that the Macedonians were *"begging us earnestly for the favor of taking part in the relief of the saints"* (2 Corinthians 8:4). They got it. They had an urgency to their giving.

Do you feel that sense of urgency? Are you proactively looking for ways to invest what God has put into your trust? Are you straining to figure out how you can give more? If so, you bear the mark of an effective steward.

### 3. Stewardship is measured by return and impact, not by what is saved.

Jesus goes to great lengths to make sure His disciples understand that stewardship is measured by the return and impact, not by what is saved. He honored how the two stewards had effectively invested what He had put into their trust and He did not honor what had been saved by the one steward.

The Master lavishes praise on the two effective stewards and gives them greater opportunity. He is truly proud of them for their effective stewardship in gaining such a great return for Him. He said nothing about how they might have saved more, but rather praised their investment savvy.

By contrast, the Master is livid with the servant who dug the hole and hid the talent, seeking to conserve what had been given to him. The Master was so furious that He took what the servant had and gave it to the best steward and then kicked the bum out!

I think a lot of Christians today define stewardship by how well people, ministries, or churches save money. My friend, *that is not good stewardship.* You can save a lot of money but fail miserably as God's steward because you have lost the opportunity for impact. That does not mean we should be foolish and irresponsible in how we spend money. But it does mean that the highest value in stewardship is not what you have saved, but how well you have used what has been entrusted to you for maximum impact.

**4. Stewardship is defined by risk, not by playing it safe.**

There are two assumptions I think we have when we read the parable of the talents in Matthew chapter 25. The first is that the two successful servants were somehow not putting the Master's money at risk. But we have to assume that there was a fairly significant level of risk. If there wasn't some risk, the third servant never would have buried his talent!

The other assumption is that this story unfolds over a fairly short period of time and that the two successful stewards got a fairly quick return on their investment. But the parable makes it clear that the Master was gone for a long time which meant there were increased variables that made the investment of the talents by the stewards a risky one.

Make no mistake about it: risk is a crucial part of stewardship. But the risk is a bit different than you might think. I think the risk in stewardship is not the potential of losing the money but rather when we invest the resources entrusted to us in what we know is right – even when it appears to be a bad financial move and reduces our personal financial position.

For example, what person in his or her right mind would believe that giving money away is a good financial decision? Human nature includes the instinct of self-preservation, so why would I give away that which brings me security?

There is a reason why philanthropy in America is driven by those who attend religious services most frequently. In fact, one study showed that those who attend religious services weekly give six times more than those who do not. And that reflects giving to all sectors of charitable organizations.

People of faith understand that investing in God's kingdom work is worth the personal risk. And they are willing to take the risk of reducing their personal financial position in order to make an investment that will have an impact and return for eternity.

But even with that I believe most Christians today do not really risk when they give. They are really, instead, playing it safe. The thought goes something like this:

*I know I'm supposed to give something, but with the mortgage, car payments, club membership, entertainment, credit card debt, expenses of raising a family, my retirement plan, and all the other expenses each month, there's just not much left to give. So I'll give, but I can't give as much as I would like with all these other expenses.*

What does that translate into? As I mentioned earlier, only 2% or so of household income in the U.S. today is being given to religious causes – by Christians.

Now the things listed above may represent entirely reasonable expenses. But this model of giving is based on the premise that only a portion of what we have belongs to God, and that is what I will give to Him each month – after I've met my other expenses.

That, however, is not the biblical model of stewardship. As we have noted earlier, true stewardship is based on an understanding that what we have is ALL His. Not just a portion. He owns it all, and He trusts us to invest all of it effectively for the best possible return for the kingdom.

THE MYTH OF STEWARDSHIP

So are we investing in stuff where rust and moth destroy? Or are we risking by focusing our investment on the eternal, where rust and moth can't touch it?

Now, don't hear me saying that a nice house, a good car, and fun vacations are not good and appropriate. They may, in fact, lead to advancing the kingdom in a very real way that makes those expenditures a great eternal investment. And God tells us in Ecclesiastes that when He gives wealth, He also gives the power to enjoy it.

But the risk of stewardship comes down to priorities.

We need to ask ourselves: "Am I so driven by gaining stuff and status … by having a 'good life' here … that I am unwilling to risk giving more of my money away to advance God's kingdom work? Have I fallen for the great seduction of the Evil One that all this stuff is more important than investing in God's glory?"

The best stewards have the Master's interests at heart, not their own, and are willing to risk their own agenda and desires to invest heavily to get the best possible return for Him.

5.  **Stewardship operates in the freedom of God's trust, not the fear of failure.**

Do you understand that God genuinely trusts you? Seriously. He trusts you with all that He has entrusted to you, otherwise He never would have given it to you.

85

This truth is affirmed in this parable where you will find the word *entrust* used three times very purposefully. This word is first used when Jesus says that the Master "entrusted" the talents into the hands of the servants. This is what He says:

> *"Again, it will be like a man going on a journey, who called his servants and entrusted his property to them. To one he gave five talents of money, to another two talents, and to another one talent, each according to his ability."*

In each case, the Master put into the trust of the servant what He knew the servant could handle. He gave each servant "according to his ability" because He knew He could trust each servant to handle that amount well.

But here is what is telling. Two of the servants believed the Master trusted them. And one did not. Here is what they say to the Master when He returns from His journey and settles accounts with them. The first servant who had been given five talents says this:

> *"'Master,' he said, 'you entrusted me with five talents. See, I have gained five more.'"*

And the servant who had been given two talents said this:

> *"'Master,' he said, 'you entrusted me with two talents; see, I have gained two more.'"*

Notice that they both used the word *entrusted.* It is the same word that the Master used when He had given the talents to the servants. In contrast, this is what the last servant said to the Master:

> "'Master,' he said, 'I knew that you are a hard man, harvesting where you have not sown and gathering where you have not scattered seed. So I was afraid and went out and hid your talent in the ground. See, here is what belongs to you.'"

This servant has a completely different mentality, a completely different worldview. This servant did not believe that the Master trusted him with what He had given to him. He operated out of a fear of failure, not the freedom of trust.

Friend, God has given you what He has given you because He trusts you to handle it well. You wouldn't have what you have if He did not *trust you.* In fact, we are reminded over and over in Scripture that it is God who gives you and me the wealth that we have (e.g., Deuteronomy 8:18; 1 Chronicles 29:10-13). And He has done so because He trusts us to handle that wealth well.

Stewardship operates in the freedom of God's trust, not in the fear of failure. The Evil One wants to hamstring you with that fear to keep you from effectively using what God has put into your trust.

6. **Stewardship is blessed by the Master with greater impact.**

At the end of the parable, we read this statement by the Master:

*"Take the talent from him and give it to the one who has the ten talents. For everyone who has will be given more, and he will have an abundance."*

God will always bless good stewardship with greater impact. If you truly want to have the greatest impact for God while here on earth, you have to be an effective steward in effectively investing the resources God has placed into your trust.

Now, it is pretty important to point out that this verse is not a pass for preaching on or believing in a prosperity gospel – the idea that if you give to God, He will bless you and make you rich. That kind of thinking misses the point all together.

Biblical stewardship is NEVER based on how much is in it for me, how much I can get from God so I can live the good life while I am here on earth. Instead, it is ALWAYS about how I can use what I have to gain more for the Master to achieve His purposes.

The servants never stopped being stewards, except for the lazy, fearful guy that buried the Master's talent. The successful stewards entered into the "happiness" of their

Master. And the Master rewarded the best steward with the talent of the one who was sent packing. Why? Because he had proven himself faithful to the Master with how well he had handled the five talents with which he had been entrusted.

Rest assured, if you steward well what God has given you, you will be given more to make an even greater impact for God's kingdom.

But let me caution you that wealth is not necessarily a sign of God's blessing. It is, in fact, a tragedy that so many Christians equate wealth and prosperity with God's blessing. If you ever wonder about that as a measurement, let me direct you to what God says to Isaiah in Isaiah 2:6-9 as but one example of Scripture's contrary testimony:

*You have abandoned your people, the house of Jacob. They are full of superstitions from the East; they practice divination like the Philistines and clasp hands with pagans. Their land is full of silver and gold; there is no end to their treasures. Their land is full of horses; there is no end to their chariots. Their land is full of idols, they bow down to the work of their hands, to what their fingers have made. So man will be brought low and mankind humbled – do not forgive them.*

Wealth is not an indication of God's blessing. In fact, God gives us a stern warning about wealth in this passage, and it is this: do not make money and wealth your idol. Do not give your heart to worshipping and following after the stuff that will ultimately disappear. God is a jealous God and will not share His glory with anything or anyone – especially money and treasures.

What this means is that the measurement of effective stewardship is not that you are necessarily going to have money overflowing, but that you will have the money *you need* to make the greatest possible impact for God's kingdom. And that is an enormous and rich promise from God.

How you steward what God has entrusted to you will directly impact the effectiveness you have for the kingdom. You cannot sidestep this issue and ignore it, just hoping it will go away. God is going to hold you accountable some day for what He has put into your trust.

Remember, we are in an all-out war against the forces of darkness and you do not win a war by skimping. You win it by effectively targeting resources for maximum impact. And that, I think, is our challenge for stewardship today.

# CHAPTER 6

# The Biblical View of Giving

NOW THAT WE HAVE LOOKED at a biblical view of stewardship we can talk about the biblical view of giving.

Giving is a delicate issue with most people. We often resist being asked for money and do not like being put on a guilt trip by someone challenging us to give. Perhaps you feel like the donor who sent the following note to a ministry with which I was once working,

> *If the Lord has truly called you to this ministry, He will supply all your needs according to His riches in glory by Christ Jesus. And if God has truly called you to ministry, He will assuredly supply all of your needs including the financial ones without you doing the fundraising.*

In other words, "Back off!" Most of us think, "Yeah! Keep your nose in your own business and exercise some faith in God! He will provide without you hounding me for money!"

But is that really true? When it comes to giving, are church and ministry and mission leaders supposed to go mute and just trust God to provide? And does the Bible inform this in any way?

Yes, it does.

In Exodus 25:2, Moses writes about the time he was on Mount Sinai in the presence of the Lord to receive the Ten Commandments. It was a Hollywood moment with the mountain blazing with the glory of God. Obviously, one of the most important moments in history.

But what Moses records as the very first words out of God's mouth is a bit shocking and incredibly telling:

> *"Tell the Israelites to bring me an offering. You are to receive the offering for me from each man whose heart prompts him to give."*

Amazing! As the preamble to giving the Ten Commandments – one of the greatest moments in human history – God begins the conversation by telling Moses how important it is for him to hold a fundraiser. He is to challenge the nation of Israel to give an offering to God to further His plan on earth.

Yes, God actually *commands* Moses to conduct a fundraiser!

And that is exactly what Moses does, as recorded in Exodus 35. He conducts the first recorded fundraising event. And in this moment, God establishes a pattern that continues through godly leaders, like David and Paul.

That pattern is this: We should expect God's appointed leaders to provide us direction and even challenge God's people to give to God's kingdom work.

Now you may be asking, "Why?" Great question.

Giving is a spiritual transaction that is a matter of the heart. As we said earlier, it is not just about the money, but about God gaining our whole-hearted devotion to Him. And if we are to be the whole-hearted followers of God that we desire to be, then we must be investing in God's kingdom work. There is no other option.

You will notice that God establishes the connection between giving and a person's heart in Exodus 25. He says that He wants His people to give with a willing and properly motivated heart. He makes clear right up front that our heart and our money are inseparable.

Another way to understand why giving to God's kingdom work is such a vital spiritual exercise is this: When we give from a willing heart, it means that we have mastery over money and it no longer has mastery over us. We are showing that money is not what we worship. It also shows our heart is given over to what matters most – God's glory and His eternal purposes.

When we hoard money, when we make it the source of our security rather than God, when we worship it by attaching greater value to it than we should . . . then it owns us and our heart, keeping God from having our whole-hearted devotion.

And Satan wins.

When we serve money, we cannot serve God. And when we put our trust in our wealth, we are not trusting God.

Before we move away from Exodus, I want you to look at something else that I think is a fascinating lesson from this passage. Notice God's timing in telling Moses to take up the offering for Him. It is right at the moment the people of Israel were taking up their own offering to build the golden calf. And guess what becomes the object of their worship?

Yes – that idol.

That is a pretty profound lesson. It gives life to the truth that Jesus teaches in Matthew 6: *where we place our treasure is where our heart will be also.* Just like the Israelites valued and worshipped the golden calf – where they had put their treasures – we will value (even worship) wherever we invest our money.

But there is more to this story. As you know, Moses destroyed the golden calf and then went back to the mountain to receive the second copy of the Ten Commandments.

When he returned, he gathered the entire nation together to set out before the people what God had told him.

In Exodus 35, we have the record of this speech. Moses followed God's command and challenged the people of Israel to give an offering to build the Tent of Meeting and to provide for the ongoing ministry that would be centered in that place. Many of the Israelites responded generously, as we read later in the chapter:

> *. . . everyone who was willing and whose heart moved him came and brought an offering to the LORD for the work on the Tent of Meeting, for all its service, and for the sacred garments* (v. 21).

Moses takes care to make sure we understand that those who gave were those whose hearts moved them. Their giving was driven by the heart and they ended up giving an enormously generous offering for God's purposes.

Mission accomplished.

Through that offering, the people advanced God's kingdom. And God got what He wanted – the hearts of the people who had given to Him and to His purposes.

In this account, I believe God establishes a precedent. It is a principle that is a Kingdom Principle for the ages. That principle is this:

> *God expects His people to give of the resources entrusted to them to make possible His plan to impact the world.*

Why? Because when the people of God fund His work, God will get what He ultimately wants – their hearts. Saying it another way, part of God's plan to win the whole-hearted devotion of His people is to make His kingdom work reliant on their support because He knows that when a person financially supports His kingdom work, that is where his or her heart will be.

Certainly, God will provide. The gentleman who wrote the letter to the ministry that I shared earlier is correct on that count. But he's wrong to think that God will somehow magically or mystically make the money appear.

God does expect His appointed leaders to challenge and motivate His people to financially support His work. And God does expect His people to respond and fund that work of ministry because that is a crucial part of gaining the whole-hearted devotion of His people.

This truth is reinforced in 1 Chronicles 29. In this chapter, David raises up contributions for the building of the temple. Verse 9 states:

> *The people rejoiced at the willing response of their leaders, for they had given freely and wholeheartedly to the LORD. David the king also rejoiced greatly.*

And then David prays the following prayer just a few verses later in verse 17:

> *I know, my God, that you test the heart and are pleased with integrity. All these things have I given*

*willingly and with honest intent. And now I have*
*seen with joy how willingly your people who are here*
*have given to you.*

God expects His people to fund His work here on earth, not just to move the ministry forward, but because giving and the heart are inseparably linked. When you and I give, it will always lead to what God really wants – *our hearts.*

So you can understand why Satan's deception is so spiritually poisonous. His effective seduction of Christians to place their trust in money rather than God blows apart the funding of God's kingdom purposes *and*, more importantly, keeps God's people from a whole-hearted devotion to Him.

## The Priority of Giving

Another passage to help us understand God's view on giving is 2 Corinthians 8. To properly grasp the importance of this chapter, we need to understand its context.

The Corinthian church was very wealthy, but it struggled to live as God desired. One might go so far as to say it was the misfit of the early Church as Paul had to constantly confront them on issues ranging from inappropriate sexual practices (including incest) to tolerating division within the body.

In 2 Corinthians 8, Paul is forced to boldly confront the Corinthians for not fulfilling a promise they had made to support the suffering church in Jerusalem. In this passage, Paul is incredibly direct with them, and even points out how stingy they are when he compares them with the churches in Macedonia. This is what he says in verses 1-4:

> *And now, brothers, we want you to know about the grace that God has given the Macedonian churches. Out of the most severe trial, their overflowing joy and their extreme poverty welled up in rich generosity. For I testify that they gave as much as they were able, and even beyond their ability. Entirely on their own, they urgently pleaded with us for the privilege of sharing in this service to the saints.*

To understand the power of this statement, you need to realize that the Macedonian church was suffering great persecution and was, in fact, *extremely* poor. Yet, in contrast to the wealthy Corinthian church, they had more than fulfilled their own commitment. In fact, they begged for the privilege of supporting their hurting brothers and ended up giving far beyond what it seemed they could, considering their poverty.

But Paul does not stop there. In verse five, he pours on the guilt when he writes that the Macedonians *"did not do as we expected* (i.e., they gave much more) ... *they gave themselves first to the Lord and then to us in keeping with God's will."*

Ouch! That had to sting the leaders of the Corinthian church. In essence, Paul is saying, "In contrast to you Corinthians, the Macedonian churches have shown that they have fully given themselves to God – they have shown that they are wholly devoted followers of Jesus Christ because of how they have so generously given to support the suffering saints in Jerusalem. On the other hand, you Corinthians have once again shown you are far from where you need to be in terms of spiritual maturity."

Paul was blunt with the Corinthian church because they needed to understand that giving was a clear indication of whether God had their heart and their genuine devotion.

Do not miss this powerful principle:

*Our stewardship of the resources God has put into our trust is a direct reflection of whether or not we have truly given ourselves to God.*

Please take a moment to think about that statement. It is one we cannot skate around. As I mentioned earlier, giving is a matter of *faith*. It demonstrates that you trust in God's provision for your needs as you follow His directive to support His work. It shows that He is the source of your security rather than your riches.

As followers of Christ, we ought to be anxious to give. We should have a sense of urgency to see God's kingdom resourced so that the battle for the souls of men, women, and children in our community, nation, and world can be advanced for God's glory.

Such a mindset begins to recalibrate how we approach giving. The question is no longer, "How much should I give?" "Should I give 10%?" Or, "should my giving amount be based on gross income or my after-tax income?"

No, the true, whole-hearted follower of Jesus Christ is all in. They do not parse giving into incremental percentages, but rather constantly ask the question, *"How much can I give?"* Like the Macedonian church, they have given themselves wholly to the Lord and out of that devotion flows generosity. And as they give, their heart devotion to God deepens.

By the way, a non-giving follower of Christ is an oxymoron. You cannot proclaim to be following Christ, to be a whole-hearted follower of Him, and not invest generously in His kingdom work. There is no such equation in Christ's kingdom.

This is such a huge issue for the Church in America and other Western cultures today. We fall far short of giving what we should, with many Christians investing little or nothing in God's work. We have fallen for the great seduction of the Evil One to make money our god.

The reality is a bit frightening. Most Christians are ignorant when it comes to understanding the vital spiritual importance of giving. In fact, as I mentioned earlier, research shows that most Christians are giving around 2% of their income and as much as 35% of Christians do not yet give at all! [4]

There is no doubt that most Christians fail to understand some basic premises:

- All we have is God's, not just 10%.
- God has entrusted us with those resources to advance His kingdom, not to use them for the primary purpose of personal gain and security.
- God's greatest desire is to have our whole-hearted devotion, yet we cannot become that kind of follower of Christ if we fail to invest our treasure in His work.

This is part of the whole counsel of God – and it is one of our Lord's major priorities. That means it should be one of yours and mine, too. Remember, it is the spiritual transaction of the heart that God cares about more than the financial transaction itself. He does not need our money; He wants our hearts!

[4] Patrick Rooney, Director of Research, Center on Philanthropy, working paper, Religious Giving presented at the Association for Research on Nonprofit Organizations and Voluntary Action, November 2007.

## The Blessing of Giving

Finally, we need to understand that biblical giving results in blessing to those who give. Nowhere in the Bible is this made clearer than in the book of Philippians.

One of the reasons Paul wrote his letter to the Philippians was to thank the Christians in Philippi for all that they had done to encourage him in his ministry and work. This included their consistent financial support of him. In Philippians 4:17, Paul writes:

*Not that I am looking for a gift, but I am looking for what may be credited to your account.*

Paul understood Christ's teaching about the proper investment of a person's treasure. If a person's investment is in kingdom work, it accrues to the benefit of the giver, being credited to his or her account. That is an eternal account, and as such it compounds for eternity. Now that is some investment! And an epic promise!

Paul also addresses the blessings that flow from giving in 2 Corinthians 9:6-11. In this passage he tells us:

*Remember this: Whoever sows sparingly will also reap sparingly, and whoever sows generously will also reap generously. Each man should give what he has decided in his heart to give, not reluctantly or under compulsion, for God loves a cheerful giver. And God is able to make all grace abound to you, so that in all things at all times, having all that you need, you will abound in every good work. As it is written: "He has scattered abroad his gifts to the poor; his righteousness endures forever." Now he who supplies seed to the sower and bread for food will also supply and increase your store of seed and will enlarge the harvest of your righteousness. You will be made rich in every way so that you can be generous on every occasion, and through us your generosity will result in thanksgiving to God.*

Paul packs a lot in these few verses, but the major theme is that God has designed giving to be a blessing to those who give. Yes, God has designed giving to bless you, not to take something away from you. It is counterintuitive to think that we gain by giving away our money, but that is the way that God's economics work.

Humanly speaking, when you and I give away money to fund God's kingdom work, it can feel as though we are making a bad financial move. After all, that is money we could use for a lot of other things. But Paul reassures us that God has our backs when we support His work. He will make sure we have what we need. And what He gives us will put us in a position to *have an abundance for every good deed* (2 Corinthians 9:8).

Paul's words echo the teaching of Jesus in Matthew 6:25-34 that we looked at earlier. God is determined to care for you. That is the heart of our Father. But Satan wants you to doubt that – to keep you from trusting God. And he uses the lure of money's false security to draw you away from trusting the Father and to instead cling to your money. That is when it becomes your god.

His lie is a subtle one: that giving our money away is something you and I cannot afford. But in God's economy, giving is not a financial loss. It is actually a gain that leads to our personal blessing. It is one of those paradoxes of God's economy that just does not make sense from the world's perspective, yet it is a principle that God has established and always validates.

*Giving always leads to blessing.* And because God has designed giving to bless us, we should approach giving with an overwhelming sense of excitement, not duty.

One of the ministries for whom we have worked for decades has one amazing donor. She is up in years and from a very wealthy family. She provides a great perspective to giving when she says, "The Lord is going first, I am just following along." Her joy is giving away the wealth God has entrusted to her!

Now, Paul is NOT saying that the blessing we will receive from giving is material prosperity. This passage does not say that you can expect some sort of financial windfall if you give to God's work. That misses the point completely. God has not designed the blessing of giving to feed a self-indulgent heart. God will not bless our giving by pouring out material blessing on us for our consumption.

What Paul is teaching is that when we give, we can be assured God will provide what we need, not what we want, with the express goal of enabling us *to have an abundance* [be abundant] *for every good deed.*

The *outflow* of giving is the blessing we receive that can come no other way. These blessings come from the hand of our infinite God and have eternal value. Sure, He may give financial blessing in the here-and-now, but Paul makes it clear that blessing is to increase our impact for His kingdom, not to live an indulgent, consumptive lifestyle.

I believe that in our day and age – especially within the societies of the Western world that are so focused on consumerism – it is tough to come into alignment with God's view of giving. We are trained to think in terms of using the money we have for personal gain, in terms of generating a return on investment in the here-and-now, and growing our portfolio to achieve greater material prosperity.

We are sucked into the consumerism of our culture with our senses dulled to the greater reality: our calling, each of us, into the intense spiritual warfare that surrounds us each moment of every day – a battle for good and for righteousness that is more than worthy of our financial participation.

Coming into alignment with God's view of giving must be a priority. It is our call as Christ-followers and children of the King to liberally and generously fund God's kingdom work by investing – with a willing heart – what God has entrusted to each of us. It is our responsibility, as followers of Christ, to use what He has given us to advance God's purposes, knowing that blessings await us that can only be measured on an eternal scale.

## Limited Resources Means Limited Impact

One of the critical understandings we must have about giving is this: If God's kingdom work is limited in its funding, it is, by definition, limited in its impact.

Clearly, the ability of a church or other Christian ministry to fulfill God's call is in direct proportion to the funding it receives to do its work. And if the devil and his forces can thwart Christians from supporting God's work, then he has won a victory in undermining the advancement and impact of God's kingdom here on earth.

Our company has an office in Australia, and on one of my trips there I had the opportunity to enjoy a private breakfast with the former head of Australia's Special Forces. This gentleman served for over 35 years in the armed forces and had a very long tenure teaching at his nation's most elite military college.

As we were discussing this issue of the funding of Christian ministry and how it is one of the areas where the spiritual battle is fiercely engaged, my friend's eyes lit up. What he went on to share both stunned and energized me.

He explained that battles are not won based on tactics, but rather on destroying the resources of the enemy. In fact, he said that this is one of the main tasks of Special Forces: to get behind enemy lines and destroy the enemy's ability to supply the troops engaged in battle.

If the enemy does not have fuel, ammunition, food, water, medical supplies – all the necessary things to wage war – they cannot fight. And if they cannot fight, they will lose the war.

That is exactly Satan's strategy! One of the things he is determined to do is to keep churches and Christian ministries from gaining the resources they need to do the work that God has called them to do. If he can do that, they, by definition, are limited in their impact. Indeed, this "scarcity maneuver" is one strategy that could have been talked about by C.S. Lewis in his masterful book about the devil's work, *The Screwtape Letters*.

I have often asked ministry leaders what they would do if they had all the money they needed. Invariably, they get a bit animated when they begin to recite the vision they would fulfill . . . *if only they had the money*!

I have watched this truth play out over and over during the decades of my work as an advisor for Christian ministries around the world. I think of one ministry that was on a handful of radio stations when we began working with them. Over the years we were able to help increase their income significantly which led to major expansion of the ministry.

Today they broadcast the gospel across the U.K., Africa, Australia, India, and the U.S. Each year they receive thousands of responses to their program, from people whose lives have been changed for eternity. One such response came from a U.K. listener:

*I feel compelled to email you and thank you for saving my life today. As with most people my story is long and complicated and I won't bore you with the details other than to say that I have suffered with poor mental health for nearly 16 years now. I've been struggling more again recently.*

*I love Jesus, but have been wondering (as countless others also) how can I be a Christian but frankly struggle with living.*

*I was listening to your programme today and while I was listening I was writing my farewell letters to my beloved husband and precious daughter, trying to explain how I was so sorry, and that I loved them so very much but I just could not find the strength to live another day.*

*I had it all planned, they are out for the day and I have the letters almost written and the pills ready.*

*Then I hear your theme tune and your voice saying "hang in there." You then recite the very chapter that I have clung to for so long, John 15, with my favourite verse... "you didn't choose me but I (Jesus) chose you."*

*That was literally 50 minutes ago, and though the tears are still flowing and the pain of depression is still very present and pressing, I have disposed of the letters and the pills and am going to cling to His nourishing vine of love and "hang in there" for another day.*

*Thank you, thank you, thank you, for your wonderful words of wisdom and that different perspective.*

The impact in this woman's life would have never been possible if it were not for the generous support of thousands of Christians. And that story has been repeated with more ministries than I can count.

But the sad part is that there is so much more that could be accomplished if only ministries had the money. Money that can only come from men and women like you and me who are committed to seeing the kingdom of God advance.

The responsibility to fund God's work in the world lies squarely on the shoulders of you and me as God's people. And He has chosen to put that mantle upon us for one reason – and it is not the money! He already owns that.

What God wants is the one thing you own and have complete control over. Your heart. And as we have seen earlier, your money and your heart are woven together in an unbreakable bond . . . which makes your heart a major battlefield for the Evil One.

# CHAPTER 7

# The Battlefield of the Heart

GOD PASSIONATELY DESIRES the whole-hearted devotion of every one of His children. The Bible is clear that this is at the top of God's agenda. Second Chronicles 16:9 says it simply and clearly:

*For the eyes of the LORD range throughout the earth to strengthen those whose hearts are fully committed to him.*

God's priority and passion is to have those whose hearts are truly and totally His. He wants your whole-hearted devotion. In fact, this is really at the core of Jesus' statement in Mark 12:30 when He beseeches us:

> *"Love the Lord your God with all your heart and with all your soul and with all your mind and with all your strength."*

God has no greater desire than to have your whole heart. God does not want to be a part of your life. He wants to *be* your life. He wants to be the affection of your heart. He wants your total and complete devotion.

God places a priority on the heart because it is the place of spiritual transaction. We are told in Scripture that salvation comes because we believe in our heart (Acts 16:31) and that faith is a matter of the heart (Proverbs 3:5-6).

The heart is the battlefield of every Christian ministry because the heart is where the spiritual battle is really waged. Accepting Jesus as Savior is a transaction of the heart. And at its core, the process of discipleship and growing people in their faith is to expand their heart for God so that God will ultimately own all of that spiritual real estate.

Knowing that the human heart is God's greatest desire, it is no wonder that Satan has made money such a vital weapon in his arsenal. He knows that if he can get you and me to treasure wealth more than God, or if he can get us to believe that money is a source of greater security than God, then God will not gain our whole heart and Satan wins. He will thwart us from fully following after God.

That is why our giving is so important. It is important for two reasons.

First, as I mentioned above, if our hearts are more intent on gaining or maintaining wealth, then we will fail to properly fund God's kingdom work. We will hold back and not invest as we should in what God is doing in the world today.

By definition, we then limit what a particular church or ministry is able to do to reach people and bring them into a personal relationship with God – or to grow believers as disciples of Christ. That means God's kingdom suffers on the spiritual battlefront.

This is one reason why, as followers of Christ, you and I must be serious in our commitment to fund God's kingdom work – whether that is through the local church or Christian para-church organizations. It is through our support that these ministries are able to advance God's purposes and win the hearts of those for whom Christ died!

But there is a second implication. And this is the one I believe most Christians do not fully understand. As noted earlier, you and I cannot truly be whole-hearted followers of God if we are not properly investing in God's kingdom work.

Remember, Jesus Himself made it abundantly clear that our money and our heart are inextricably tied together.

How we view and value money and what we do with money have everything to do with whether God has our whole heart. And if having the whole heart of His children is God's deepest desire, then He cares a lot about how we steward the money He has entrusted to us.

Let me say this again, because it is so important.

*You and I cannot be wholly devoted to God if we are not investing our money in His Kingdom work because our hearts follow wherever we invest our money!*

So when we as God's people are driven to and committed to fund His work, not only do we advance God's kingdom plan to win the hearts of men, women, and children and grow their hearts into a deeper devotion to Him, but God gets our hearts as well.

And your whole-hearted devotion to God is the last thing Satan wants.

So you can understand why Satan is so actively resisting and thwarting the funding of God's kingdom here on earth. He not only wants to undermine God's work by limiting the resources a church or para-church organization has to fund its work, he also wants to keep you and every other believer from giving his or her whole heart to God.

You can see why giving is indeed a critical part of growing in our walk with Christ. When we give to God's work, we do not just fund that work, we align our hearts with what God is doing in the world today and we increase the devotion of our heart to Him. That is what giving is really all about.

# CHAPTER 8

# All In: The Only Source of Real Security

IT WAS TWO O'CLOCK in the morning. I awoke to the sounds of muffled talk and the quiet beeping of machines. Except for a sliver of light from the door, the room was pitch-black.

I felt awful. The radioactive iodine was doing its work to rid my body of any remaining cancer cells. And while there was no physical pain, I just remember thinking that this is what death must feel like.

As I lay there unable to go back to sleep, I felt a different kind of pain – one I had never felt before. It came from the lack of any human contact for more than 50 hours. I was literally radioactive, with yellow caution tape on the floor of my room indicating where no one was allowed to pass. I was now going on day three of isolation.

I never thought that such seclusion could be so intensely painful.

Worse than that, it felt like God was nowhere to be found in that darkness. Try as I might to reach out to Him, God was silent. It was the lowest moment of my life. Why would He not show up? I could use some encouragement, some hope. Something . . . anything!

Silence. Darkness. And just muffled voices and a few beeps from some distant machines.

There are no words to describe the utter despair I felt in that moment as I lay there in the dark, struggling with the pain and loneliness of an isolation I had never known, with the sense that God was nowhere to be found and the knowledge that no one – not even a nurse! – could come close to me. I heard a small whisper, a voice speaking into my heart:

*Imagine an eternity of this, Rick.*

I could not. "This is what hell must be like," I thought. The weight of that thought just crushed my soul.

In that moment, God completed the work He had begun three months earlier when I had been diagnosed with thyroid cancer. And I knew I would never look at life the same way again. No, I would never be the same.

Through my cancer I had looked death in the face and now, three months later, God had given me the most incredible gift: *a new perspective on life.*

As I look back, I now see what He was doing. As I shared at the beginning of this book, I had been fired from my first job out of seminary and my wife and I had lost nearly everything. He had stripped away any pretense I had about being able to control my own destiny and showed me that life was about more than the stuff our culture throws at us as the measure of happiness and success.

Then, 20 years later, God took us once again to the brink of losing everything to show us that only He could ever be the source of our security or peace – that God, and only God, could be trusted to provide the security for which every human heart is made to long.

And then, just six months later, I was fighting cancer, coming face to face with my own mortality. The lesson? *Our lives are not about the here-and-now. This is not our reality but a momentary sliver of time in which we live.*

Instead, you and I have been placed into an epic saga… a story of God's relentless pursuit to redeem His creation from the grip of the Evil One, releasing us from the bondage of sin and death which have separated us from Him. God is on a mission to destroy forever the stranglehold of Satan's dominion and power over this world.

And He has called you and me, His people, to make that mission our priority.

This saga is being played out in the spiritual realm where Satan will do all he can to thwart God's plan, with consequences impacting every human being. We have abundant evidence that he has declared an all-out war on Christ and His followers. Yet, most of us live as though no battle exists. We pursue a life of happiness, leisure, comfort, and fortune, often oblivious to the reality of the spirit realm and its impact on our every moment. We live as though we have no clue that all around us the battle rages every moment with innumerable causalities. Because more often than not, we are, in fact, clueless to this reality.

If you doubt what I am saying, let me remind you of the call to battle issued by the apostle Paul in Ephesians 6:10-13 where he writes to us:

*Finally, be strong in the Lord and in his mighty power. Put on the full armor of God so that you can take your stand against the devil's schemes. For our struggle is not against flesh and blood, but against the rulers, against the authorities, against the powers of this dark world and against the spiritual forces of evil in the heavenly realms. Therefore put on the full armor of God, so that when the day of evil comes, you may be able to stand your ground, and after you have done everything, to stand.*

The spiritual forces of evil are active every moment of every day pursuing their agenda and executing their plan to thwart God's kingdom. This has a dire impact on the physical realm in which you and I live. That is why Paul does not say *if* the day of evil comes, but *when.*

For whatever reason, we fail to realize that we are on Satan's turf. As the prince of this world, he is pretty upset about God advancing on his territory; so he is unleashing the full force of his power against God's kingdom, which includes you and me as Christ-followers.

Jesus made a point of reminding His disciples that they were in enemy territory at the end of the Last Supper. He told His disciples, *"I will no longer talk much with you, for the ruler of this world is coming ..."* (John 14:30, ESV). And when He prays for the disciples at the end of the supper, Jesus asks the Father not to take them out of the world, but to protect them from the Evil One.

Wow. Of anything He could have prayed, the fact that His disciples were being left in enemy territory was foremost on Jesus' mind. Which is why He prayed that God would protect them from Satan himself.

This world continues under Satan's rule today. In 1 John 5:19, John says it quite plainly:

> *We know that we are children of God, and that the whole world is under the control of the evil one.*

Paul provides the same insight in 2 Corinthians 4:3-4 when he states:

> *And even if our gospel is veiled, it is veiled to those who are perishing. The god of this age has blinded the minds of unbelievers, so that they cannot see the light of the gospel of the glory of Christ, who is the image of God.*

Satan is the god of this world and he is actively opposing God's desire to see men and women come to know Jesus Christ. We know that we are on his turf and Satan and his forces are on the offensive. Every day. Every hour. And one of his main strategies is to seduce you, me, and every other believer with the allure of money's power. To make it our god. To deceive us into believing that it can bring the security that only God can bring, keeping our hearts from fully following after God and His eternal purposes. And doing all he can to keep us from investing in it to resource the advancement of God's kingdom here on earth.

Make no mistake: the devil wants to keep you from being all in for the battle of men and women's souls by ensuring your devotion to money and the false security it brings. He wants nothing more than for you to put greater value in money than you should and beat a hasty retreat from investing in God's kingdom program.

Check out the parable of the soils as recorded in Matthew 13:18-23:

> *"Listen then to what the parable of the sower means: When anyone hears the message about the kingdom and does not understand it, the evil one comes and snatches away what was sown in his heart. This is the seed sown along the path. The one who received the seed that fell on rocky places is the man who hears the word and at once receives it with joy. But since he has no root, he lasts only a short time. When trouble or persecution comes because of the word, he quickly falls away.* **The one who received the seed that fell among the thorns is the man who hears the word, but the worries of this life and the deceitfulness of wealth choke it, making it unfruitful.** *But the one who received the seed that fell on good soil is the man who hears the word and understands it. He produces a crop, yielding a hundred, sixty or thirty times what was sown"* (emphasis mine).

You cannot help but notice what Jesus says in verse 19 – that Satan is actively thwarting the spread of the gospel. But what I want you to really focus on is what Jesus says in verse 22, the portion I have emphasized above. It sounds like Jesus knew our generation and what would cause us to be unfruitful.

*The one who received the seed that fell among the*

*thorns is the man who hears the word, but the worries of this life and the deceitfulness of wealth choke it, making it unfruitful.*

How you handle your money is at the core of your fruitfulness as a believer. If money and possessions are your priority, you have fallen into the trap laid for you by the devil. You will never be a whole-hearted follower of Jesus Christ and you will be unfruitful. *And Satan wins by keeping you from your rightful place on the front lines of the spiritual battle.*

It is little wonder Jesus spent so much time driving home the reality of this truth through His parables. Earlier we looked at Luke's account of the parable of the rich fool. Look at the entire passage in Luke 12:13-34, as it gives direct insight into how Jesus views money, stuff, and where we should place our priorities:

*Someone in the crowd said to him, "Teacher, tell my brother to divide the inheritance with me." Jesus replied, "Man, who appointed me a judge or an arbiter between you?" Then he said to them, "Watch out! Be on your guard against all kinds of greed; a man's life does not consist in the abundance of his possessions."*

*And he told them this parable: "The ground of a certain rich man produced a good crop. He thought to himself, 'What shall I do? I have no room to store my crops.' Then he said, 'This is what I'll do. I will tear down my barns and build bigger ones, and there I will store all my grain and my goods. And I'll say to myself, "You have plenty of good things laid up for many years. Take life easy; eat, drink, and be merry."' But God said to him, 'You fool! This very night your life will be demanded from you. Then who will get what you have prepared for yourself?' This is how it will be with anyone who stores up things for himself but is not rich toward God."*

*Then Jesus said to His disciples: "Therefore I tell you, do not worry about your life, what you will eat; or about your body, what you will wear. Life is more than food, and the body more than clothes. Consider the ravens: They do not sow or reap, they have no storeroom or barn; yet God feeds them. And how much more valuable you are than birds! Who of you by worrying can add a single hour to his life? Since you cannot do this very little thing, why do you worry about the rest? Consider how the lilies grow. They do not labor or spin. Yet I tell you, not even Solomon in all his splendor was dressed like one of these. If that is how God clothes the grass of the field, which is here today, and tomorrow is thrown into the fire, how much more will he clothe you, O you of little faith!*

*"And do not set your heart on what you will eat or drink; do not worry about it. For the pagan world runs after all such things, and your Father knows that you need them. But seek his kingdom, and these things will be given to you as well.*

*"Do not be afraid, little flock, for your Father has been pleased to give you the kingdom. Sell your possessions and give to the poor. Provide purses for yourselves that will not wear out, a treasure in heaven that will not be exhausted, where no thief comes near and no moth destroys. For where your treasure is, there your heart will be also."*

The family member had a reasonable beef. His brother owed him his part of the inheritance. But Jesus redirected the issue. He knew the human heart and the tendency to covet money and things. So Jesus used this as a teachable moment. His points were clear and so applicable to us today:

- You are a fool if you focus on accumulating wealth but are not rich toward God. In other words, you are to be pitied if your priority isn't on how you invest what God has given you for eternal purposes, but on using your money for self-serving purposes of ever-increasing storehouses of wealth.
- You need to understand that God is a more secure source of provision than your money!

- You should be a committed giver to God's kingdom purposes so you can build a storehouse of treasure that will NEVER be depleted or destroyed!
- You should understand that where you put your treasure is where you will put your affection and what will own your heart.

It is this last point that is the real kicker and where you and I need to get serious. Jesus never says (nor do we find it anywhere in the New Testament): "Where your time is, there your heart will be also." He never says it about our prayer life, the amount of time we spend in Bible study, our marriage, our personal relationships, or any other thing in life. Yet, that is what we emphasize most in our churches today.

The only thing Jesus ever says is a driver to where our heart will be is – *our treasure.*

Maybe that is why He was so harsh with the church at Laodicea. In Revelation 3:14-19, Jesus says this to that church:

> *"To the angel of the church in Laodicea write: These are the words of the Amen, the faithful and true witness, the ruler of God's creation. I know your deeds, that you are neither cold nor hot. I wish you were either one or the other! So, because you are lukewarm—neither hot nor cold—I am about to*

*spit you out of my mouth. You say, 'I am rich; I have acquired wealth and do not need a thing.' But you do not realize that you are wretched, pitiful, poor, blind and naked. I counsel you to buy from me gold refined in the fire, so you can become rich; and white clothes to wear, so you can cover your shameful nakedness; and salve to put on your eyes, so you can see. Those whom I love I rebuke and discipline. So be earnest, and repent."*

Wow. It is easy to read this dispassionately, but the language makes it clear that our Lord is angry. And I do not know about you, but the last thing I would ever want is to have Jesus look me in the eyes and rebuke me so harshly.

Jesus is ready to *vomit* these Christians out of His mouth because they are so lukewarm in their faith. Yes, *vomit* is the literal translation of the word. And why is He so nauseated? Because these Christians are so wealthy they believe they have no need of anything – *not even God.*

They have made their priority the accumulation of wealth and have done an amazing job of that, so amazing that their wealth had masked the fact that they were spiritually destitute. And it makes Jesus want to throw up.

What is the solution? Jesus says, *"Buy from me gold refined in the fire, so you can become rich; and white clothes to wear so you can cover your shameful nakedness; and salve to put on your eyes so you can see."* In other words, take the wealth you have and invest in the things that are God's, those things that will last for eternity!

My fear is that the Church in America and other countries in the developed world is like the church in Laodicea. Financially wealthy, but spiritually destitute.

But there is another church that Scripture applauds for how it invests in kingdom work. It is the church at Macedonia which we looked at earlier. Take a look again at what the apostle Paul says about them in 2 Corinthians 8:1-5:

> *And now, brothers, we want you to know about the grace that God has given the Macedonian churches. Out of the most severe trial, their overflowing joy and their extreme poverty welled up in rich generosity. For I testify that they gave as much as they were able, and even beyond their ability. Entirely on their own, they urgently pleaded with us for the privilege of sharing in this service to the saints. And they did not do as we expected, but they gave themselves first to the Lord and then to us in keeping with God's will.*

What a contrast to the church at Laodicea. The Macedonians were far from rich. They struggled through severe persecution and deep poverty, yet their response was to beg for the privilege of giving to God's kingdom purposes.

My question to you today is this: *Are you a Laodicean or Macedonian?* Is your financial priority taking care of yourself or seeing God's kingdom advanced?

You can claim that you desire to follow God with all your heart, but your financial priorities will indicate whether that is true or not. You are not really following after God if you are not committed to making your giving to kingdom purposes a priority. Without that fundamental commitment, you are not a whole-hearted follower of Christ! It is impossible.

Regardless of what the world might say, regardless of the state of the markets, regardless of what our cultural value system might thrust our way, you and I need to be resolute in our determination to make God's kingdom our financial priority. The stuff of the here-and-now will always disappear and always fail to deliver what our society says it will. You and I need to put first the advancement of the gospel through how we use what God has entrusted to us, including our support of the local church and Christian ministries.

What we do with our treasure proves where our heart really is. It shows if we are truly in the battle. It is irrefutable evidence of whether or not we are whole-hearted followers of Jesus Christ, fully devoted to the cause of Christ, wanting to see men and women moved from darkness to light – from the power of Satan to God.

At the end of his rebuke of the Laodicean church, Jesus makes this admonition:

*Those whom I love I rebuke and discipline. So be earnest, and repent. Here I am! I stand at the door and knock. If anyone hears my voice and opens the door, I will come in and eat with him, and he with me.*

Yes, Jesus was mad at the trap of materialism that the Laodicean church had fallen into. But His grace prevails. He was ready to throw-up at the shallowness of their faith, but His heart yearns for them ... and for us ... to know Him and be wholly His. To let Him come and care for us as only He can.

If you feel you need to make some adjustments after reading this book, Jesus wants you to know He is not condemning you. He is ***admonishing*** you to turn from those false and hollow promises of money and wealth and find your security in Him and Him alone. He's ready and waiting for that deep and intimate relationship with you.

So what do you do? Let me give you three points to consider:

- If you are enslaved to consumer debt, especially credit card debt, make it your top priority to erase that debt. That means taking measures to first stop any further accumulation of debt and then putting a disciplined plan in place to get out from under that financial bondage.

- Have you overextended yourself? Maybe that means you acquired a car that in reality is above your means. If so, perhaps you need to go to the dealer to see what kind of a deal you can negotiate to get into something that more reasonably fits your pay grade. The same thing applies to your home or any other possession. Yes, God empowers you to enjoy the wealth He gives you, but if you live under the constant financial pressure of being overextended, then it begs the question of whether your financial priorities are God's financial priorities.

- What is your commitment to giving to fund God's kingdom purposes, starting with your local church? And how does that relate to the rest of your financial expenditures? If you are not giving, start. Set an amount for each pay period or month and stick to it. Do not worry about the percentage, especially if you are in debt. God is not about guilting you into giving. He wants giving that comes from a cheerful heart. My opinion is that God will be most honored for you to get out of debt first, but do give something as you do – and take it off the top, not after you have paid everything else. If you are giving, take time to evaluate it against your other financial priorities and ask God for the wisdom to help you make it an increasing financial commitment.

Today, God wants you to know true financial freedom. He wants you to live in the genuine security of His care, fully trusting Him (not your portfolio) to provide for you. He wants to help you break free from the bondage of the Evil One who has you trapped in a financial corner. And in that freedom and security, He calls you to live a life that is all out for Him, for His glory, and for the advancing of His kingdom.

Maybe today you find yourself under immense financial pressure. You are stretched so thin you feel like you are ready to break at any time. The toll on your family has been immense – and even greater on your marriage. Striving to get ahead, to live the dream, has become a burden that feels like a 10-ton weight that is slowly but surely crushing you. You just do not know how much more you can take.

If this describes you, there is no question that you are living under one of the most powerful deceptions of the Evil One. And one of the lies he has used to trick you into striving so hard to gain wealth is the lie that God cannot be trusted for your security. You cannot really rest in Him. He just is not all that concerned about you as an individual.

You sense the invasive power of the conflict that Jesus described in John 10:10 when He declared:

> *"The thief comes only to steal and kill and destroy; I have come that you may have life, and have it to the full."*

So stop believing Satan's lies. Instead, respond today to the words of Jesus in Matthew 11:28-30:

> *"Come to me, all you who are weary and burdened, and I will give you rest. Take my yoke upon you and learn from me, for I am gentle and humble in heart, and you will find rest for your souls. For my yoke is easy and my burden is light."*

This is the heart of our God. He stands before you with arms wide open. He wants you to stop striving for what will never satisfy and, instead, find your rest and security in Him! He wants you to place your full trust in Him and begin the journey of giving Him your whole-hearted devotion.

When you look to God and begin to fully trust Him to care for you, you will know what it means to be secure. *Truly secure.*

But the only way to get there is to trust Him fully by making His kingdom your financial priority, treasuring up treasures in heaven and not living for the here-and-now. That is when He will have your whole heart and you will really know what it means to be *secure.*

# CHAPTER 9

# Now What?

OK. SO YOU GET IT. You understand that your only true source of security is found in Jesus and His commitment to care for you. That life is not about the stuff of the here-and-now, but about a much bigger play. You know you're a part of an epic spiritual struggle for the hearts of men and women, with eternal consequences.

You also get that God has placed you into this struggle with resources to invest in His kingdom work – to see His kingdom advanced. And that your heart will follow after whatever you do with what He has put into your trust. If you invest in the stuff of the earth, your heart will follow the temporal. But if you invest your stuff into the things of the kingdom, your heart will follow Jesus and what Jesus really cares about – the eternal.

So now what? How do you begin to step into the new way of thinking? Let me give you a biblical framework that I hope will help.

## Your Perspective

It starts with your perspective, which is summed up in one of the most important passages of Scripture, Galatians 2:20. It reads:

> *I have been crucified with Christ; and it is no longer I who live, but Christ lives in me; and the life which I now live in the flesh I live by faith in the Son of God, who loved me and gave Himself up for me.* (NASB)

You are dead. Yep, your former life that was bound to the stuff of this earth is gone. This former life is the life that Paul described in Ephesians 2:1-3:

> *As for you, you were dead in your transgressions and sins, in which you used to live when you followed the ways of this world and of the ruler of the kingdom of the air, the spirit who is now at work in those who are disobedient. All of us also lived among them at one time, gratifying the cravings of our sinful nature and following its desires and thoughts. Like the rest, we were by nature objects of wrath.*

You were spiritually dead, living a life following after the desires and priorities of this world. A life under the authority of Satan. And it was that life which was crucified with Christ. Now, Christ Himself, through the Holy Spirit, lives in you.

What an amazing thought – a true mystery.

This is the central truth of the New Covenant: ***that God Himself would live in us***. As Paul says in Colossians 1:26-27,

> … *the mystery that has been kept hidden for ages and generations, but is now disclosed to the saints. To them God has chosen to make known among the Gentiles the glorious riches of this mystery, **which is Christ in you**, the hope of glory.*

Jesus Christ, through the Holy Spirit, resides in you. This is the mystery that God has kept hidden for ages, but has now revealed to us. It's been God's plan all along to place His Holy Spirit in His people – the Spirit of the resurrected Christ!

Now His passion is to live His life ***through*** you.

I want you to pause for a moment and let this sink in. Jesus is alive in you and now wants to live ***through*** you. This is Paul's point in Galatians 5 when he talks about the fruit of the Spirit. That fruit is evidence of the Holy Spirit living through you, of you being led by the Spirit.

But Paul says there is one condition to this life, and that is faith. Trusting Jesus to, in fact, live His life *through* you! That's why Paul makes a point to say in Galatians 2:20 that he not only recognizes he was crucified with Christ and that Christ now lives in him, but, "The life I live in the body, I live *by faith* in the Son of God, who loved me and gave himself for me."

You don't have to beg Christ to live His life through you. That's His passion and plan. But you can stifle Him from doing that by not trusting Him to do so. That's why Paul admonishes us in 1 Thessalonians 5:19 to not quench the Spirit, because He can be quenched.

This life we live is a life of faith, trusting God to live through us. When we do, we give priority to living by the guidance and truth He reveals in Scripture. As we exercise that faith, He then empowers us to live that way. That's why He sent His Holy Spirit. He knew we would need His supernatural power to live the life He has for us. As He told His disciples just before He left earth:

> *"But you will receive power when the Holy Spirit comes on you; and you will be my witnesses in Jerusalem, and in all Judea and Samaria, and to the ends of the earth"* (Acts 1:8).

That's Christ in you! And He's there to live His life through you in His power!

Sometimes we fear abandoning ourselves in a radical way to God. We get caught up in the what-ifs and become convinced that He's going to take our lives in a direction we don't want. Or isn't in our best interest.

That's a lie and deception straight from the pit of hell.

You can fully trust Jesus because He has proven conclusively that He has your best interest at heart. He jumped in front of the wrath of God aimed at you and took the hit for you. And now He wants you to trust Him to lead you and live through you.

This issue of trust is why getting the money thing right is so important. Because money is at the core of who and what you trust. If you trust your wealth rather than Christ for your security – for your life – your heart is not fully God's and you stifle the ability for Christ to live through you. You quench the Spirit. You will fail to fulfill your eternal destiny as you keep Christ from empowering you and living through you as He wants.

But if you grasp this truth that Christ is guaranteeing your security and you can trust Him to live His life through you, it will color your perspective on all of life. You can step into each day in the freedom, peace, and security of knowing that Jesus is alive in you, doing His thing. You have this incredible source of power, wisdom, and grace living through you.

So it starts with the right perspective, which then leads to the understanding that you indeed have a purpose.

## Your Purpose

As Jesus lives His life through you, He has a plan. Each day is not some random series of events, some sort of spontaneous reaction to each day. There's a plan with a specific purpose and focus. Paul says it this way in Ephesians 2:10:

> *For we are God's handiwork, created in Christ Jesus to do good works, which God prepared in advance for us to do.*

It's a pretty incredible thought that God, in eternity past, thoughtfully prepared a plan for you. It's deliberate and crafted around whom He has made you to be. It's something you can fulfill. And it's good. Really good.

Jesus put it this way in John 15:7-8:

> *"If you remain in me and my words remain in you, ask whatever you wish, and it will be done for you. This is to my Father's glory, **that you bear much fruit**, showing yourselves to be my disciples."*

And in John 10:10, Jesus said it as plainly as possible:

> *"The thief comes only to steal and kill and destroy; I came that they may have life, and have it abundantly."* (NASB)

God's passionate desire is for your life to be full, abundant, and fruitful. This brings Him great glory and is part of His plan. He's rooting for you to live out the life He has thoughtfully prepared for you – a life that is rich and rewarding. A life that comes from being in Christ, which you are if you're a follower of Christ, and Him living in you.

This fruitfulness is the mark of success for the Christian – not the accumulation of wealth, status, and power that the world sets as the evidence of success.

So do you want to live a fruitful life? A REALLY fruitful life? Well, God has that wired for you, but you need to embrace the truth that Christ is in you and wants to live His life through you. And you must trust Him to do so. If you do, you release Him to put into play the plan He has designed for you.

This obviously has implications for all of life. But the question I want to address is how this affects the stewardship of your wealth.

## Your Priority

As Jesus lives His life through you, He has a driving priority for what you do with the stuff He has put into your trust. This priority is revealed in an ancient truth, disclosed thousands of years ago. It's captured in Genesis 12:2-3, when God commissioned Abraham to His purpose:

*"I will make you into a great nation and I will bless you; I will make your name great, and you will be a blessing. I will bless those who bless you, and whoever curses you I will curse; and all peoples on earth will be blessed through you."*

God tells Abraham that He has a plan for him. That plan is to make him into a great nation through which Abraham will bless "all peoples on earth." God would bless Abraham so He could be a blessing.

This is always God's plan: To bless His people so they can bless others. God blesses you and me to bless others. The apostle Paul puts it this way in 2 Corinthians 9:8:

*God is able to bless you abundantly, so that in all things at all times, having all that you need, you will abound in every good work.*

When Paul talks about "blessing you abundantly," the word he uses is the word for grace. He uses grace as a synonym for money, as in this passage he is referring specifically to money. In 2 Corinthians 8:1, Paul talks about the "grace" that God had given the Macedonian church. That grace was the ability to bless the saints in Jerusalem through financial support, which they desperately needed.

So, too, Paul says that God will cause this grace to "abound" to you and me so we have all we need and can abound in blessing others. In fact, that's the whole point of the ninth chapter of 2 Corinthians. Paul wants the Corinthians to understand that God has blessed them to be a blessing. Their giving to support the saints in Jerusalem shouldn't be a burden, but a natural, cheerful outflowing of the grace God has poured into their lives. And when that happens, praise and glory flow to God.

God has poured blessing into your life for the purpose of blessing others. It doesn't mean He hasn't given you the power to enjoy what He has given you. We saw earlier that when God gives wealth, He also gives the power to enjoy it. But it doesn't stop there. He gives the blessing of wealth ultimately to bless others – to abound in "good works."

Let me put it another way. Jesus wants to bless others through you. Through the power of His Spirit living in you, He wants to use you to bless others – to express His love for them through you.

So as you step into this life of trusting God for your security and you reorient your finances around kingdom priorities, know that God has given you what you have in order to bless others. You are blessed to be a blessing.

That blessing may come directly or indirectly. Directly blessing others may be helping a neighbor, friend, or relative who is going through a rough patch right now. Maybe it's picking up the tab for a couple across the restaurant who are obviously counting pennies, or buying coffee for the person next to you in line at Starbucks. It could be giving the waitress an extra-large tip or taking the single mom who's struggling to the grocery store. There are an infinite number of ways to directly bless others if you have that as a priority of your stewardship.

You can also indirectly bless others through your support of a myriad of organizations. It starts with your support of your local church and its effort to build the body of Christ. Beyond that there are numerous Christian organizations that are reaching into your community, spreading the gospel around the world, feeding the poor, rescuing women from human trafficking, helping those caught in the grip of drug and alcohol abuse, fighting for social justice. Again, the opportunities are almost limitless – if your framework of understanding is that you've been blessed to be a blessing.

My point is this: When you come to realize that God has given you favor and blessing so that He can bless others through you – and that this is part of the plan for an abundant and fulfilling life He designed for you in eternity past – it changes how you look at wealth, money, and the stuff of the here-and-now.

You can be sure this truth is sinking in when you move away from a lifestyle of consumerism and materialism that is burdened by:

- the weight of debt

- the unfulfilling pursuit of status
- the chronic emptiness that comes from never having enough
- the unholy fear of the future
- the unhealthy concern about what others think of you, and
- the decay of self-absorption

These maladies are replaced instead by a life that rests in the freedom, joy, and peace of the security you have in Christ, the power of Him living through you, and an insatiable passion to live for the things of eternity – the things that matter. You step into each day with a consciousness of the epic spiritual struggle all around you knowing that God has placed you – yes, *you* – into the midst of that battle for a very specific purpose. And you will fulfill that purpose as Christ, not money, has your heart and Christ lives through you. As He does, He will touch your heart to want to bless others as He has blessed you.

When it comes to money and wealth, you know you've been blessed to be a blessing.

Now, stop reading and step into the life God has designed for you. By faith, abandon your life and future to Him. And trust Him to live through you to unfold day by day His plan for your life – that abundant, fruitful life that is marked by blessing others as you are blessed.

# Faithful
### is He who calls YOU, WHO also will do it.

1 Thessalonians 5:24

Heaven is a place where we shall never sin; where we shall cease our constant watch against an indefatigable enemy, because there will be no tempter to snare our feet. There the wicked cease from troubling, and the weary are at rest. Heaven is the "undefiled inheritance"; it is the land of perfect holiness, and therefore of complete security.

But do not the saints even on earth sometimes taste the joys of blissful security? The doctrine of God's Word is, that all who are in union with the Lamb are safe; that all the righteous shall hold on their way; that those who have committed their souls to the keeping of Christ shall find Him a faithful and immutable preserver. Sustained by such a doctrine we can enjoy security even on earth; not that high and glorious security which renders us free from every slip; but that holy security which arises from the sure promise of Jesus that none who believe in Him shall ever perish, but shall be with Him where He is.

Believer, let us often reflect with joy on the doctrine of the perseverance of the saints, and honor the faithfulness of our God by a holy confidence in Him.

May our God bring home to you a sense of your safety in Christ Jesus! May He assure you that your name is graven on His hand; and whisper in your ear the promise, "Fear not, for I am with thee." Look upon Him, the great Surety of the covenant, as faithful and true, and, therefore, bound and engaged to present you, the weakest of the family, with all the chosen race, before the throne of God; and in such a sweet contemplation you will drink the juice of the spiced wine of the Lord's pomegranate, and taste the dainty fruits of Paradise. You will have an antepast of the enjoyments which ravish the souls of the perfect saints above, if you can believe with unstaggering faith that "faithful is He that calleth you, who also will do it."

– Charles Haddon Spurgeon (in *Morning by Morning*)

www.TheSecureBook.com

The Life<sup>n</sup> Books Collection
consists of short, topical readers
about the making of a well-lived life.

(Created for people who seek
*a life of uncommon yield.*)

**Other Titles in the Life<sup>n</sup> Books Collection**

*The Ultimate Gift*
by Jim Stovall
[STEWARDSHIP]

*A Peace of My Mind*
by Stuart Briscoe
[PEACE]

*HANDOFF*
by Jeff Myers
[MENTORING]

*The Manhattan Declaration*
Foreword by Charles Colson,
with Other Commentary
[CULTURE-MAKING]

**www.life-n.com**